Lives That Speak

Stories of Twentieth-Century Quakers

by the
Religious Education
Committee of
Friends General Conference

Marnie Clark, editor

ISBN 1-888305-32-0

Book design and composition by David Budmen

Front cover illustration: *The March on Washington: A View of the Rally from the Reflecting Pool* by Nat Herz (photograph by Nat Herz, © Barbara Singer, www.barbarasinger.com, New York, NY).

Back cover illustrations (top to bottom): Bayard Rustin, courtesy of Swarthmore College Peace Collection, Swarthmore, PA; Elise Boulding, courtesy of Elise Boulding; Gordon Hirabayashi, courtesy of *Friends Journal*; Barbara Reynolds with Japanese woman, courtesy of Wilmington College Peace Resource Center.

Library of Congress Cataloging-in-Publication Data
Lives that speak : stories of twentieth-century Quakers / by the Religious
Education Committee of Friends General Conference.—1st ed.
    p. cm.
   ISBN 1-888305-32-0 (alk. paper)
   1. Quakers—Biography—Juvenile literature. I. Friends General Conference
(U.S.). Religious Education Committee.

BX7791.L52 2004
289.6′092′2—dc22

                                                          2004001514

For further information about this publication
and other Quaker resources, please contact:

    Friends General Conference
    1216 Arch Street, 2B
    Philadelphia, PA 19107
    215-561-1700
    Or find us at www.quaker.org/fgc

To order this or other publications call 800-966-4556,
e-mail bookstore@fgc.quaker.org or you can order from us on the web at
www.quakerbooks.org.

Contents

Preface

Quakerism is not just a faith but a way of being in the world. A central tenet of Quakerism is the importance of having our lives be an expression of our testimonies. This collection of stories is about Friends whose lives have spoken their faith loudly and clearly.

In preparing these stories, we wanted to affirm the message of the title—that our lives—our choices and our interactions in the world—tell who we really are. We also thought it was important for Quaker children to see Quakerism as something that is happening now, not just something that happened in the time of George Fox or William Penn. In our own times, there are many Quakers whose lives are speaking in a wide variety of resourceful ways. We have chosen sixteen men and women to highlight. We hope these stories will help children consider ways their own lives can speak.

This is a revision of an earlier curriculum called *Lives That Speak* that was published jointly by Friends United Meeting and Friends General Conference. The earlier collection contained thirteen stories about Friends with an emphasis on missions. They ranged from Mary Fisher's story in the seventeenth century to Herbert Hoover's in the twentieth. The curriculum contained a teacher's manual and leaflets for three different age groups.

This time our format is a story book with a few questions and suggested activities for teachers and parents to use in helping children identify with the people in the stories and think more deeply about how they were meeting the challenges in their lives. The stories are written for upper elementary children, roughly fourth to eighth grades. Many of the activities call for searches by computer or in the library to broaden the information in the stories.

Role models are important for children. They help children learn what is possible and admirable. The role models we offer in these stories would be of limited value if they were paragons with virtues unattainable for most of us. It is clear that the Friends in these stories have seen themselves as very fallible, ordinary folks who had struggles and made mistakes. The important thing was that they developed a passion for service and witness that enabled them to do things they hadn't known they could do.

These stories show how sixteen Friends—eight women and eight men—have responded to problems and challenges of our time with courage and creativity and caring. Many of the stories describe experiences and contacts in childhood that led to the person's adult direction and commitment. To round out the picture, we have also included short accounts of the four Nobel Prize awards to Quakers. We begin with encouragement to look for people in their own meetings whose "lives speak."

All these people, in their own ways, have heard and responded to Margaret Fell's challenge: "So-and-so said this or that. What canst *thou* say?"

How is the Spirit moving in *your* life?

EDITORIAL COMMITTEE:
Marnie Clark, Convenor
Jeanette Baker
Katie McCorkle
Melissa Meyer
Beth Parrish
Barbara Robinson
Suzanne Siverling

Introduction
Finding "lives that speak" in Our Meetings

by Beth Parrish

I sang *Amazing Grace* in meeting for worship one day and commented that although I didn't feel quite like the "wretch" in the song, I was aware that there were many things to which I was no longer blind. After meeting, during introductions and sharing time, Paul Adams shared about the time he remembered hearing African Americans sing, "was bound but now I'm free" instead of "was blind but now I see."

The next week after meeting, Ellen Neville shared some history of the writer of *Amazing Grace*. He had captured and sold slaves from Africa but later realized how wrong he had been to treat people that way and wrote the song.

When I think of the people who attend our meeting, I realize how many could be included in this volume of *Lives That Speak*.

- Carrie Christensen, in her twenties and teaching about peaceful conflict resolution in our First Day School, majored in peace studies in college. Part of that study included teaching school children in riot-ridden Northern Ireland to deal constructively with conflict.
- Roger Geeslin brings concerns about human rights and the environment from his work with the Quaker United Nations Program.

- Lee Thomas shares about business ethics and business organization. He promoted civil rights and marched with Dr. Martin Luther King, Jr. He shares with our First Day School about that and about how awful war is.
- Katrina Kearfott, a physician at a clinic for low-income people, lobbied for a healthcare system that would better meet the needs of everyone. She talked about her disappointment in not achieving that goal.

Each person I have gotten to know has a story to tell. How do I learn about people in my meeting? I listen. I observe. I take time to ask questions. We have forums during which people tell about their journeys and special concerns.

In preparing the stories in this book, there were several questions we asked each person, whenever it was possible to do so:

- How do you want your life to speak?
- How does this relate to your Quaker faith?
- How did this passion or direction develop?
- What childhood influences were important?
- What specific experiences or events in your life do you feel express your life message?

In your own meeting, you can ask these same kinds of questions. You may be surprised to discover that people you thought weren't unusual at all have had some amazing life journeys. You might start out by asking what led them to Quakerism or how the Inner Light has affected their life. Or you might want to know other kinds of things, such as where they grew up or how they have faced danger and fear in their lives.

There are so many questions you might ask, and their answers will lead you to other questions. You won't know what you've been missing till you ask. Then you may want to record the adventure of that person's life in a written story or on a tape (audio or video) to share with First Day School classes and with others in your meeting.

Stephen L. Angell
Trusting Leadings

by Johanna Anderson

Have you ever met a person who is so excited about what they are doing that their whole face seems to light up when they tell you about it? They might seem quiet and shy at first. Then, they start to talk to you about something that is very special to them and it seems that the more they think and talk about it the more energized they become.

Steve Angell is this kind of person. He is a Quaker who is passionate about peace and has been for as long as he can remember. If you want to see his face light up like a Christmas tree, all you have to do is get him to tell you about the leadings that have guided him to the work he does today. Steve works for an organization called the Alternatives to Violence Project (AVP).[1] He has taken the work of this organization to communities all over this country and throughout the world. When he is leading an AVP workshop, Steve seems to have enough joyful energy to fill an entire room.

Steve Angell in his 70s.

[1] Steve was part of a small group in New York Yearly Meeting that started the Alternatives to Violence Project (AVP).

When I asked Steve how he first became interested in peacemaking, he said, "Oh, that is an easy question to answer. I was very fortunate. I had some strong leadings early on in my life. I was very young when I had my first one." I asked if he remembered what his early leadings felt like and he answered, "Sure I do. They are not the kind of experiences you are likely to forget."

Beginnings

Steve was born in 1919. He was the youngest of three boys in a close and loving family. Steve was named for his father; he also had an uncle whose name was Steve—Steve Holden. His dad and his uncle were very strong influences on him as he was growing up.

The Angells lived in Scarsdale, New York, and the Holdens lived in nearby White Plains. Steve remembers many happy times playing with his two older brothers and his Holden

Steve and his brothers (he is the youngest one).

cousins. The Angells and the Holdens celebrated holidays as one big family, and they vacationed together in the summertime.

Steve did not start out as a Quaker but there were Quaker influences in his family. In the old days, Steve's great-grandfather had been a Quaker but had been read out of his meeting for marrying someone who was not a Quaker. Steve explained the custom this way. "They did not kick my great-grandfather out the door or anything. He just couldn't do any of the work of the meeting after that. He couldn't be clerk or work on any of the committees of his meeting, but he continued to attend meeting for worship for the rest of his life."

In Steve's early years, his family attended a Congregational Church. Steve says, "I liked the music, but I was fidgety during the services. They just didn't speak to me." Meanwhile, the Holdens, who had also attended the Congregational Church, began to attend an unprogrammed Quaker meeting when they were on vacation. One summer, the Holdens invited Steve's family to come with them. After that, the Angell family began to attend the meeting in Scarsdale. From the first, Steve felt comfortable with unprogrammed worship. "It felt like coming home. It felt so good, in fact, that I have been going ever since."

Early Leadings

Steve was about five when he had his first experience of a leading of the spirit. "I call these experiences awakenings" he explains.

> I was born just after World War I. When adults spoke of this war they called it "the war to end all war." One night when I was about five or six years old I was lying in my bed thinking about the soldiers in the trenches who were shooting at one another, and trying to kill one another. I felt that I wanted to stand up and say to them, "This doesn't make any sense. Let's go home." Even though I was so young at the time, I had a strong, clear sense that I just could not accept the idea that war was an answer. I wanted to find another way.

Another leading came when Steve was about ten or so. His older brothers were beginning to discuss their ideas for future careers. Steve's father had a successful business in real estate, and it was becoming clear that the older brothers were going to pursue other paths. It was only natural that Steve's dad would look to him as the son who would follow in his footsteps. Steve would have been well suited for that kind of work. He was a friendly and outgoing boy. He enjoyed meeting people, and he liked being part of a community. He enjoyed going from door to door to sell tickets for a good cause.

Steve was aware of his father's hopes and expectations, but he was also beginning to get a clear sense that he was meant to do something else in his life. One day, this realization came to him so clearly that it made him feel very sad. His parents were concerned when they found him crying. Steve explained that he didn't want to disappoint his father but he just knew he was not meant to go into the real estate business. His parents listened to him and encouraged him to find his own path.

Steve's parents became very involved in their new meeting and participated every summer in New York Yearly Meeting which was held in Manhattan in those days. Steve remembers that being part of the larger Quaker community was lots of fun. Beds were set up in classrooms at the Quaker Seminary in Manhattan. There were programs for the adults and special activities for children of all ages, and there was a separate program for the high schoolers.

Steve as a Boy Scout.

Steve also became involved in the Boy Scouts. His scout leaders realized that he had many skills that would make him a good teacher or counselor, and he was given many opportunities to develop those gifts. When he was ready for college, he decided that he wanted to study to be a social worker. He was especially interested in working to build and strengthen communities.

Meanwhile, he had not forgotten his earliest leading, against war. At this time World War II was on the horizon and all US male citizens between 18 and 26 were subject to being drafted into the army. When he was eighteen, he wrote a letter to his draft board. In it, he explained that his conscience would not permit him to fight in a war. He asked to be registered as a conscientious objector—a CO. The draft board in Scarsdale was not ready to have a CO in their community, but they tried to find some other way to keep Steve from having to serve in the military. He was a strong and healthy young man, but they classified him as 4F. That was a classification for people who had serious health problems. Steve had athlete's foot!

A Conscientious Objector and a Worker for Peace

When World War II began, Steve was just beginning his masters program. He wanted to make his opposition to the war clear so he reapplied to the Scarsdale draft board. This time, with the help of an excellent draft counselor, Mr. Allee, he was able to register as a CO. Instead of military service, COs were assigned to do other service useful to the country. For his alternative service, he did social work.

When the war ended Steve returned to school to complete his masters degree. He found out that his draft counselor had a daughter, Barbara, who was just about his age. Barbara was working for the American Friends Service Committee at the time. Steve says that it was love at first sight. Steve and Barbara were married and eventually had four children. Through the years, Steve continued to work as a social worker and continued to be involved in the Quaker community, working for peace and fairness in society.

During the 1940s, the Friends Committee on National Legislation (FCNL) was founded. One of its main goals is to free the world from war and the fear of war. It's special focus was on educating members of congress. Steve dedicated himself to the work of this organization and served as its clerk for nine years. It was during this time that Steve had one of the most powerful leadings of his life.

Saying No, Then Yes

Early in 1970, the Vietnam War was going on and President Nixon was in the White House. Steve and his family had moved to a farm in order to reduce their family income enough to avoid paying federal income taxes because their taxes would support the war. One day, Steve heard a radio announcement that Dr. Norman Vincent Peale, Nixon's spiritual advisor, was going to have open office hours that day at his church in New York City and anyone who wanted to could come and speak with him. Steve felt a leading which actually felt like a message to go, and it gave him some difficulty.

He tells the story like this,

> I got a message that I should go and see Dr. Peale and talk to him about his support of President Nixon's conduct of the war in Vietnam. I tried to put this out of my mind as something I didn't want to do. I was actually on the subway when the hour came and I had no conflicting appointments. I could easily have continued to the proper subway stop and gone in to see Dr. Peale, but I refused to do so. This left me feeling extremely uncomfortable, so uncomfortable that I finally said, "Please let me off this time. If you let me off this time, I PROMISE if you ever again ask me to do something like this, I will do it."

The next time came a few months later. In June 1970, the national news was much worse. Four students had been killed by the National Guard at Kent State University during an anti-war demonstration. In Washington, DC, on the weekend after the killings, the largest anti-war demonstration so far took place. On this same weekend, Steve had appointments in Washington for his consulting business. Also, he was to attend a committee meeting at FCNL.

Steve was listening to the news on his car radio as he was approaching Washington. This is how he tells what happened next:

> I was very much focused on my travel progress and getting to Washington in time for my one o'clock appointment and all seemed to be going well. It was at this time that I got a message. The message was that I should go to Camp David and give a message to the president. First of all, I had no idea how to get to Camp David, and second, I did not know what the message was that I should give to the president. This had to be a whole bunch of nonsense, I thought, and I kept trying to put it out of my mind, but it would not let me go of me.

Steve found himself just listening and following directions that led him to Catoctin National Park and to a road with a sign marked "Camp David." When he saw this sign, he was so overwhelmed that he had to pull over to the side of the road to compose himself. In a few minutes, there was an officer sitting in his car listening to Steve tell his story of why he was at Camp David and how he had managed to get there.

He came to the part of the story where he was supposed to tell what his message was for Nixon. All this time he had had no clue what that message might be. His feelings and opinions of the president had been very negative, but as he began speaking about this to the officer, he found himself experiencing compassion for Nixon. He was able to feel empathy for the weight of the president's concerns and responsibilities during this difficult time. He was led to say that at 11:00 AM.

the Quakers and others would be holding a meeting for worship in Lafayette Park, in back of the White House, to pray for Nixon, that he might be well guided in the decisions that he had to make.

Steve has never again had a leading so powerful as this one, but his life was changed by this experience. He now knows from his own experience that there is a power that can give direction to his life. Since that time Steve has been even more focussed in his efforts on work for peace.

In the 1980s, a great change came over Steve's life when his wife Barbara died. He decided to dedicate himself fully to the work of the Alternatives to Violence Project and this is where you will find him today. Since his wife Barbara died in 1988, he has devoted himself to the task of taking the message of AVP all over the world. He sees AVP as a pro-

The AVP Mandala, designed by Steve Angell.

gram with a message of peace for people and communities in every part of the planet. In AVP, Steve Angell feels that he has found a way to fulfill his lifelong dream for a peaceful path.

Going Deeper

Questions to Ponder

1. How does Steve's life speak to you?
2. Have you ever felt a leading of the Spirit yourself? Can you describe the experience?

3. Whom do you know that seems to be living a Spirit-led life? How can you tell?
4. How do you feel about conscientious objection to war?

Activities

1. Find out more about the Alternatives to Violence Project at the library or on the internet (**AVPUSA.org**). AVP/USA, 1050 Selby Avenue, St. Paul, MI 55104. Telephone: 877-926-8287.
2. Contact AVP and arrange for someone to give a talk or a workshop.
3. Invite a member of your meeting to visit your class to talk about leadings.

Illustration Credits

All illustrations for this chapter courtesy of Stephen L. Angell.

Elise Boulding
World Peacemaker

by Mary Lee Morrison

E lise was very worried. It was 1940, during World War II, and the German Nazi army had just invaded and occupied Norway. Norway was the country Elise had left seventeen years earlier when she and her parents had left to move to the United States, when Elise was three years old. Elise's mother, Birgit, had always been unhappy about leaving Norway. She kept alive in Elise's mind a vision of Norway as a safe, secure, beautiful place, a place to which Elise could return some day if she wished.

Now Elise realized that Norway was no longer safe or secure. She knew she could not return any time soon, and that made her sad. It also made her think about how many places in the world were no longer safe because of the war. She worried about all of the people who would suffer—families who would lose people they loved and homes and towns that would be destroyed. Right then and there, as a twenty-year old

Elise in her late 70s.

college student, Elise decided that working for peace and
world security would be her life's work. For Elise this was an
epiphany, an event that marked a major turning point for her.

Elise's parents named her Elise Biöm Hansen. She was the
eldest of three sisters. The family was very close and lived in a
place in New Jersey where there were many other immigrant
families from Norway. Her family spoke Norwegian at home,
but Elise learned to speak English at school. Here is what she
says about an early memory, probably from soon after her
arrival in the United States.

> I was standing on the sidewalk surrounded by a circle of kids
> who were all speaking things I couldn't understand (they were
> speaking English). They were all completely incomprehensible
> to me, I just have that one memory standing there listening to
> all this jabber that made no sense to me. I wasn't frightened. It
> was just a puzzle!

This memory helps us understand why as a child Elise often
felt that she was "on the outside looking in." She believes that
being an immigrant was very helpful for her, though, because
it made her more able to understand things from two very different perspectives, American and Norwegian. Her ability to be
part of two cultures, "standing with one foot in each" as she
says, helped her greatly later during her career as a sociologist.
She studied the ways individuals and groups work for peace.
Elise, from a very early age, recognized how it is possible for
people looking at the same situation to see it very differently.

Even as a young child, Elise recognized injustice and felt
that it was her duty to stand against it. Here is what she
remembers about an incident in her schoolyard when she was
in elementary school:

> I remember when the boys were teasing the girls and I was
> taller than the other girls. I can remember just standing in
> front of the girls, protecting them from the boys and just
> telling the boys off (she laughs as she tells this).

As a small child, Elise greatly enjoyed nature and the out-of-doors. "The circle of trees in our yard was my playhouse," she remembers. She would climb one of the trees and sit in the branches with her paper dolls, making up stories about the dolls and inventing plays. She especially enjoyed the quiet and solitude she found there, sitting by herself among the trees. Later she would remember that these special times and places of solitude helped her to feel God's presence.

Elise when she graduated from Douglas College, 1940.

After she had children of her own, she wrote a pamphlet about how important it is for children to have a chance for solitude.

After college, Elise lived for a short time in New York City. Here she began attending Quaker meeting occasionally, encouraged by the Friends she had met who were fellow musicians. Elise played the cello.

Turning Point

After she moved to Syracuse, New York, to attend graduate school, she began attending meeting there more regularly. One day, she was attending a quarterly meeting of Quakers held in Syracuse, when she met a young Englishman named Kenneth Boulding who was teaching economics at Colgate University. He was also a poet. Elise recognized immediately what a special person Kenneth was, with his keen mind and brilliant ability to put ideas and words together in unexpected ways. Elise says that meeting Kenneth was another epiphany for her, another major turning point in her life.

Elise felt that God had brought them together. They were engaged three weeks later and married the next year in a Quaker ceremony. She joined the Religious Society of Friends about the same time.

A Small Plot of Heaven

When they were married, Elise and Kenneth pledged to make their home and family life "a small plot of heaven." They wanted their home to be full of love and a place where their children could grow up learning how to be peacemakers.

Within the space of eight years five Boulding children were born—four boys and a girl. Elise stayed home to care for the children and became very much involved in the children's schools and in the meeting's First Day School, helping both teachers and children learn how important peace is. She began writing pamphlets and curricula that were used in many Quaker meetings. She also helped get books celebrating peace into libraries and worked to get rid of toys that encouraged violence and warlike thinking.

Expanding Horizons

Elise took advantage of a chance to travel to the Soviet Union and to other countries that were regarded at that time as enemies of the United States. On these visits she brought messages of hope and love to schools and community groups. She felt it was important to speak out about how dangerous it could be to talk about people as "enemies." She believed that such talk could lead to thinking that would promote a culture valuing war.

Soon after she was married, she began to study how the United Nations could help make the world more peaceful and secure. The United Nations was new then. It had been started just after the end of World War II with high hopes that it might prevent future wars. Elise was excited about its potential and especially interested in what ordinary citizens could do to help its work.

Besides the General Assembly, in which all member nations have a vote, and the Security Council, which has fifteen members and the power to deal with special crises, Elise found that there are many special agencies associated with the United Nations that work to make life better for the world's people in special ways. Three of these are the World Health Organization, the World Food Organization, and United Nations Children's Fund (UNICEF), which helps children all over the world.

The Importance of Non-Governmental Organizations

Elise learned that many organizations she knew about, like the Boy and Girl Scouts, the YMCA and YWCA, and the Friends World Committee for Consultation are also connected with the United Nations. Because they are citizen organizations, not part of any government, they are called non-governmental organizations (NGOs). Many have national or international leaders who are able to attend sessions of the United Nations agencies and make suggestions. Some NGOs work to provide food, some to improve education or family planning, some to build wells or teach better farming methods. All these activities help to build a more peaceful and safe world.

As she learned more about NGOs, Elise became convinced that people do not have to travel around the world to work for peace. Ordinary people can work for peace right at home.

For example, a person who joins a local chapter of the Scouts or Amnesty International or the World Federalists is automatically connnected with people doing the same kind of work in chapters of the same organization in other countries. That makes them all part of a worldwide movement toward a peaceful, strong society. Even when the members never meet each other in person, they can feel their connection, realizing that they are all parts of a larger effort toward a more peaceful world. Sometimes they are in close touch with each other and have regular conferences where they share with one another what they are doing.

When Elise helped out with her children's Brownie and Scout activities, she would always point out that the children were part of a world culture, not just members of their own troop. When she began to teach in college, she would ask her students to name all the NGOs they had taken part in and think about how these were helping to build world peace.

Peacemaking Skills Start at Home

Elise believes that families can play an important part in building peace. It is in families that peacemaking skills are first learned if children and adults learn to listen to one another and practice mutually respectful negotiation on a daily basis. She thinks the greatest gift that children give parents is recognition of the need for sensitivity to another person's needs and the capacity to see the world freshly. She believes that separating children by age levels at school is unfortunate because children miss out on opportunities to learn from older and younger children. Sometimes Quaker meetings are the only places where children learn to know people of other ages.

As her children were growing up, Elise became involved in many local organizations, often as a leader. During the early years of her activism the Bouldings were living in Ann Arbor, Michigan, where Kenneth was teaching economics at the University of Michigan. Elise continued to play the cello until she became so busy with childrearing, writing, and speaking for peace that she found little time to play.

Elise was also becoming a popular lecturer at Quaker gatherings. Sometimes she and Kenneth would speak or lead workshops together. Although their personalities and teaching styles were very different, they had a close partnership in working for peace.

By 1966 Elise and Kenneth and many other Quakers were becoming alarmed about the role of the United States government in the war in Vietnam. Feeling that more people needed to be speaking out and witnessing against it, Elise decided to run for a seat in the United States Congress from her district in Michigan. She ran as an independent candidate on a peace ticket. She did not win, but she believes it was important that she entered the race, as someone speaking out against the war and the suffering it was causing on all sides.

As her children grew up, Elise traveled more, soon becoming a leader in national and international organizations. One of these was the Women's International League for Peace and Freedom (WILPF).

Teaching, Speaking, Writing, and Serving in the Government

Elise had begun to teach sociology at the college level. At least once, however, when she was almost hired for a job, the university decided to hire someone who held a doctoral degree instead of Elise. Anticipating other limitations on her progress, she decided to go back to school to earn a doctorate in sociology. After she received it, her world traveling for peace increased.

In 1967 the Bouldings moved to Boulder, Colorado. Elise was forty-seven years old and her children were now teenagers and young adults. Both she and Kenneth taught at the University of Colorado, and several years later Elise became head of the Sociology Department at Dartmouth College, where she started a program to study peace.

Over the next thirty years, Elise would become well known for her scholarship and writings on peace. She saw her special mission as bringing together teachers and those who were studying and acting for peace, whether through vigiling, writing, or speaking, giving each a chance to listen to other points of view, thus enhancing their own understanding and effectiveness.

In 1979 President Jimmy Carter appointed Elise as a commissioner to help establish the United States Institute for Peace. For two years, Elise and her fellow commissioners listened to people's ideas about how to organize such an agency. Then they testified before the United States Congress, urging it to establish an Institute of Peace. They were successful: the United States Institute of Peace was set up. Its mission is to promote the peaceful resolution of international conflicts. During this time, Elise also became an advisor to the UN-sponsored World University in Japan.

After Kenneth died in 1993, Elise moved to Massachusetts to live near her daughter Christine. She transferred her membership from Boulder, Colorado to the Wellesley Friends Meeting and soon completed a book she had begun earlier about cultures of peace. In this book, *Cultures of Peace, the Hidden Side of History*, she reported results of the many years of studying, speaking, and writing that she had begun years earlier on ways to build peace. She finished this book in part because the United Nations General Assembly had declared the years 2000–2010 as a "Decade for a Culture of Peace and Nonviolence for the Children of the World." Elise dedicated her book to "A Culture of Peace."

Elise also helped begin the Friends Peace Teams Project. This group has sent peacemakers to several parts of the world. For example, one team of Quakers from Africa and the United States was sent to Burundi to help heal the wounds and trauma caused by many years of civil war. They have helped in part, by giving victims of that violence opportunities to tell their stories and listen to the stories of others.

Visualizing Peace

Elise believes that imagining peace is one of the best ways we can make progress in working for it and that children and young people can often imagine peace better than adults. She has conducted workshops in which people, both young and old, are asked to create in their minds and describe in detail what the world might look like if everyone had enough food, shelter, and love, and if there were no wars. This visioning begins with walking through a thick, imaginary "hedge" into the world of the future, where the world is at peace. What does this world look like? What are people doing in it? How are they relating to one another?

After participants have imagined and described this future world in detail, they are challenged to imagine the steps that might have led to such a peaceful world. Finally, they plan the first steps that they can take now.

In all the traveling, writing and speaking for peace that she has done in all her work as a teacher and activist, Elise has never forgotten what she learned from her years of being with children. She believes that children can teach adults important lessons about play—about how to have fun—and about how important it is to listen to one another. She challenges us to use that creativity to envision a more peaceful world and then to act on our vision. We can begin to do this in our communities, in our Quaker meetings, and right in our very own homes.

Going Deeper

Questions to Ponder

1. How does Elise's life speak to you?
2. Have you ever had an experience of way opening—where you changed your mind about the basic direction you wanted to follow in your life?
3. Growing up Elise often felt as if she was "on the outside, looking in." When have you felt like an outsider?
4. How have you (or people you know) worked together with people from other backgrounds for a common goal?

Activities

1. Find the US Institute for Peace online or at the library. What does this organization do?
2. Plan and carry out a visit to another Quaker meeting or worship group; maybe plan a picnic or other activity together. Explore with them whether and how both groups might work toward peace and justice.
3. Find out what resources are available in your community to work for peace and justice?

Illustration Credits

Both illustrations for this chapter courtesy of Elise Boulding.

Calhoun Geiger
Quiet Courage

by Carol Passmore

In 1917, when Calhoun Geiger (pronounced gee-ger) was born, the state of Florida did not have a large population. Big towns had electricity but no air conditioning. Florida was a hot place to live. Cal and his five brothers and sisters lived on their family farm near Jacksonville. They helped their parents raise most of the food for the family. They also grew food for their animals—chickens, cows, sheep, and a mule. They cut wood for the stove and cut wood to sell.

The school was five miles away. The school bus was a wagon pulled by a mule. Going to school would have meant leaving home early in the morning and getting home after dark. Cal's parents thought there were more important things to do (like chores) than have long rides in a wagon every day. So Cal and his brothers and sisters did not go to school. Their parents taught all six children at home. Besides work and home

Cal as a young man.

school, the children had time for fun. They went camping and swimming and built a boat. They played games and had fun with neighbors and relatives who lived nearby.

Another thing Cal did not do was go to church. His parents didn't think church was important. But they lived in a way based on the teachings of the Bible. In fact, Bible study was a part of every day's lessons in the Geigers' home school. The things that Cal learned in his Bible study turned out to be the things that Quakers believe.

Becoming a Conscientious Objector

When Cal was very young, he admired his uncles who had fought in World War I. He thought he might like to wear a uniform some day. But when he was in his late teens, he met a young Methodist minister and began to attend the Methodist Church. Cal had learned the Bible so well that he was soon teaching a Sunday School class of men much older than he was. He enjoyed talking to the minister about religious questions. In the 1930s, as people in the United States began talking about a coming war, Cal remembered the verses he had learned:

Blessed are the peacemakers. (Matt.5:9)

Love your enemies, do good to those who hate you and spitefully use you. (Luke 6:27–28)

Cal came to realize that his conscience would not let him be a soldier. He knew he could not kill another human being. His brother and two cousins felt the same way. They all registered as conscientious objectors (COs). Their draft board did not question the sincerity of their belief that it is wrong to kill. As COs, they would be assigned to non-military service "of national importance."

When the war came, Cal's first assignment as a CO was to Buck Creek Gap, North Carolina, where COs were building campgrounds on the Blue Ridge Parkway. They were also on call to fight any forest fires that might start in the area. In this work, Cal met Vernon Barber, the first Quaker he had ever known. Cal had heard about William Penn but had not known any Quakers living in the twentieth century. Cal was pleased that Vernon Barber could tell him about Quakers.

Because Cal was a forester and loved to be outdoors, he enjoyed his work at Buck Creek Gap. He wondered, though, if it was important to be building campgrounds when a war was going on. Because of the war, people could not buy gas or tires, so no one could come to the new campgrounds anyway.

Seeking That of God in Mental Patients

When a call came for COs to work in mental hospitals, Cal and his brother volunteered. The mental hospital in Williamsburg, Virginia, where they were sent, was very old— even older than the United States. It had been started before the American Revolution. The COs who worked there found that not very much had changed about either the buildings or the way patients were treated. Life there was very difficult for both the patients and the COs.

Patients were treated roughly at the hospital. One staff member told Cal, "They are all dangerous; that's why they are locked up. The only way to be safe is to keep them afraid of us." But Cal was not afraid of the patients. He saw each one as a person, and he was confident that he would find "that of God" in each one. He also saw each patient as a possible friend. He was kind to the patients and they grew to like and trust him.

Soon Cal was assigned to night duty, working from 6 at night till 6 in the morning with the most disturbed patients. This was a hard and dangerous assignment, which Cal was given because he was big and strong. He didn't use his physical strength to control the patients, though. One night, he heard a patient humming a hymn. Cal hummed along. The patient hummed louder and so did Cal. They decided that maybe some of the other patients would like to sing too. Soon the whole ward was singing hymns. Every night after chores were done, they all sang and then the patients went quietly off to bed.

Cal and the other COs found ways to make life better for the patients at the mental hospital. They had a fire drill for the first time that anyone could remember and discovered that some doors could not be opened. Although the COs were scolded for having the fire drill, all the old rusted locks were quickly replaced. When the COs told the newspapers about the lack of medical treatment for patients, the medical care improved.

The years Cal spent at the mental hospital were very important to him. He met many other COs and learned more about Quaker beliefs. Once he was chosen to travel to Washington to make a report about the work the COs were doing at the mental hospital. He also went to Pendle Hill, a Quaker conference center, where he met Rufus Jones and other Quaker leaders.

Farming and Helping

When Cal finished his alternative service in 1946, he returned home to Florida. He had been writing to his girl, Virgie Peake, the whole time he was away. When he got home, they married and built a little house. Cal was glad to be able to take up farming and timbering again. He thought often about the mental hospital and the work he had done there, but he didn't plan to quit farming. Then one day, as he crossed a road on his farm, a car slowed down. The driver was a juvenile court judge and a friend of Cal's family. After they talked a few minutes, the judge said, "Now Calhoun, I think it is time for you to quit spending all your time growing pine trees, corn, taters, and sugar cane—and come help me work with troubled kids." Cal realized that this was the right step for him and soon he was working for the Jacksonville Boys Club, organizing activities for needy boys.

While Cal was working for the Boys Club, his daughter Ileen was born and later two sons, Glenn and Edward. He and Virgie and a few other interested people started a Friends meeting in Jacksonville. One person who came to the meeting was a Girl Scout leader. Girl Scouts were strictly segregated in Florida in the early 1950s. There was a camp for white Scouts, but black Scouts could not ever use it, so the camp was often empty. Cal and others from the meeting worked to build a camp for black Scouts. But Cal also kept suggesting that the two groups of girls scouts should work together.

When the Girl Scouts' annual meeting was being planned, the leaders agreed that Cal was right. For the first time, black and white Scouts had their annual meeting together and performed on the stage together. As a result of Cal's efforts, the camps and several troops were integrated. Someone who did not want integration burned a cross on the lawn of Cal and Virgie's house, but the Girl Scouts of America named Cal "man of the year."

Cal and the Commander

Cal enjoyed his work at the Boys Club, but he was uncomfortable that so many of the activities involved the military and included visits to the Naval Air Station near Jacksonville. One time the boys were invited to spend the day on the *USS Lake Chaplain*, an aircraft carrier, while it was in port. Cal went to the ship to make arrangements for the visit.

When it was time for lunch, Cal was at the table with the commander of the ship. The ship's doctor was also at the table. He asked Cal, "Were you in the navy?" Some of us might have tried to avoid the question, but not Cal.

"No," he answered. "I'm one of those odd people who think there are better ways than war to solve problems."

"Oh, were you a conscientious objector?" the doctor asked.

Cal said that he was and answered the doctor's many questions about why he was a CO. He realized that the commander was listening to the conversation, but he didn't hesitate to say what he believed. A few days later, Cal brought 437 boys to spend the day on the aircraft carrier.

A few months later Cal received first a letter and then a phone call from the American Friends Service Committee (AFSC) asking if he would be interested in working for them. Here was Cal's chance to leave the militaristic Boys Club. He went to Philadelphia for an interview. He was most amazed to learn that the commander of the aircraft carrier had recommended him to the AFSC. The commander had written a letter saying that he had been very moved by listening to Cal. He knew about the AFSC from a Quaker sailor. He felt Cal would be a valuable worker for the AFSC. Cal was probably the only person recommended to the AFSC, a peace organization, by a military officer.

Cal worked for the AFSC on peace issues, including draft counseling, and on racial integration in the High Point, NC, office. After that he worked at Arthur Morgan School and then at Quaker Lake Conference Center. His last job was at Carolina Friends School in Durham, where he enjoyed working with children in a school based on Quaker beliefs.

Cal always worked quietly and showed his faith in the way he lived. He influenced many people and has many stories to tell. The one that has always fascinated people the most is the story of Cal and the prisoner.

Cal and the Prisoner

Cal was in his field plowing one day while a group of prisoners, wearing striped uniforms and being guarded by men with guns, were working on the road nearby. Cal stopped to grease the bearings on his plow. Suddenly, he looked up and found that a prisoner had escaped through the hedge and was standing over him with a club." I need money awful bad, and I'm going to take whatever you have," said the man.

Cal knew he couldn't run away or overpower the man with the club. He said, "If you need help that badly, why don't you just say so, and we won't have any rough stuff about it." Meanwhile, Cal continued greasing his plow bearings.

The escaped prisoner didn't know what to do with a man who wouldn't fight. He lowered the club a little. Cal talked to him about running away and reminded him that he would be a hunted man. Suddenly, the prisoner said, "You win. I'm going back" and disappeared into the bushes. Cal did not know for sure whether the man went back.

But that is not the end of the story. Five years later, when Cal was working for the Boys Club, he was driving home from a meeting one evening. He saw two cars crash into each other. The drivers were not hurt, but they got out of their cars and began to fight. One man fell to the ground and the other man began to kick him and hit him with a wrench.

Cal wanted to drive by and not get involved, but he heard an inner voice telling him to stop so he did. The voice reminded him that he was a strong man, so he wrapped his arms around the man who was kicking the other man. They fell to the ground but Cal held on to him. Someone else called the police, who soon came with plenty of handcuffs. They wanted to handcuff Cal too until he explained what had happened so they let him go. It was dark and Cal never saw the faces of the two men.

But that is not the end of the story either. One day when Cal was doing volunteer work in a mental hospital, a hospital worker told Cal that a man named George Harris wanted to give him a gift. Cal did not remember anyone named George Harris. The worker said that George was the escaped prisoner and also the driver of the car. If Cal had not stopped him,

George would be a murderer. George had been a patient in that hospital where Cal was volunteering and had learned his name. Now he was well and had a steady job. He wouldn't come to meet Cal, but sent him an expensive watch, which kept good time for fifty years.

In the years that followed, as Cal moved around, George kept track of where he was and sent him many gifts, including a pair of leather boots just the right size and a wood worker's bench. Then one day when Cal was working at Carolina Friends School, an old man drove up and got out of his car. He went to Cal and introduced himself as George Harris. He was ill and wanted to thank Cal in person before he died.

Just before he died, George Harris dictated a letter to his wife about how Cal had saved his life. One First Day when friends came to the Durham Meeting, they found the letter. It ended with these instructions to his wife: "When you get through writing it (the letter) up, send it to Cal's friends in Durham. I want them to know all about the humble, hard-working man that is among them. Thank God for Cal Geiger."

Going Deeper

Questions to Ponder

1. How does Cal's life speak to you?
2. How would your life be different if TV and computers didn't exist?
3. What steps led to Cal's becoming a CO?
4. In what ways is your community integrated? In what ways is it segregated?

Activities

1. Find out what kinds of work prisoners do in your state. Are they paid? How do you feel about prisoners having to work?

2. Ask someone who regularly visits in prison to come and talk about his/her experiences.

3. Find someone in your meeting who was a conscientious objector and invite him to visit your class to talk about his experience.

Illustration Credits

The illustration for this chapter courtesy of Calhoun Geiger.

Gordon Hirabayashi
Idealism Is Realism

by Marnie Clark

Imagine that you are a young college student in Seattle and a member of the local Quaker meeting. You are a US citizen because you were born in this country. You love the United States and are proud to belong to a country with a constitution that protects its citizens. Your parents are not citizens because Japanese immigrants are not allowed to become citizens or even to own land in this country. They would have become naturalized citizens long ago if it had been possible, for they love this country too.

One peaceful Sunday just after meeting for worship, someone turns on a radio and hears the news that Japanese planes have bombed Pearl Harbor in Hawaii and sunk a lot of ships there. Many people have been killed. The next day the announcement comes that the United States has declared war on Japan.

Soon a curfew is announced. All people of Japanese, German, or Italian ancestry must be off the street between 8 PM and 6 AM. All three groups are now regarded

Gordon Hirabayashi.

as wartime enemies. (The United States has already been helping the British in their war against Germany and Italy. Now it will enter the European war too.)

A little later, notices appear on telephone poles and post office bulletin boards around Seattle. They say that all people of Japanese ancestry who live near the coast will be moved inland to detention centers. They may take only two suitcases apiece with them and must sell or store everything else they own.

Although the curfew applies to all three "wartime enemy" groups, this new order is just for people of Japanese ancestry—"both alien and non-alien." By "non-alien" they mean US citizens, but they don't like to admit that they're doing this to US citizens so they call them "non-aliens." Maybe other citizens won't notice.

At least two-thirds of the people who will be taken away are citizens! The government also tries to make it sound better by calling it "evacuation" instead of "forced removal" and saying it's to "detention centers" instead of to "concentration camps."

Suppose you believe this order is wrong—not only unfair and misleading but illegal under the constitution. The courts are still functioning. Martial law has not been declared. Arresting people without a specific accusation and holding them without a trial is a violation of rights guaranteed by the constitution. You are only a student and you don't know much about the law, but you do know that much.

Japanese families on their way to a detention camp.

All the Japanese-Americans you know are obeying the curfew and getting ready to leave when they are ordered to do so. They feel terribly humiliated, and they will lose everything they have been working for and saving, but they want to show their loyalty to their country. They think following the government's order is the patriotic thing to do.

All the time you were growing up you felt a lot of prejudice against Japanese people, but it's much worse now. There is a hysterical fear that the Japanese army may be getting ready to invade California and that Japanese living on the West Coast may help them and sabotage the US defenses.

What do you do?

What would you do in a situation like that? Would you think you even had a choice?

What One Man Did

This is how Gordon Hirabayashi, a young US-born son of Japanese parents and a member of the Seattle Friends Meeting, explains what he did.

My reaction developed in three stages. At first I obeyed the curfew. My friends would remind me, "Hey, Gordie, it's five to eight." and I would dash back to my room. But then I began to think, "I'm an American citizen!" So I decided to act like other citizens. I stopped obeying the curfew.

I was still assuming I would obey the "evacuation" order when it came. I didn't sign up for spring classes. Instead I volunteered with the American Friends Service Committee while I was waiting. One of my duties was to help Japanese-American families get ready to leave, especially some families whose fathers had been arrested by the FBI right after the Pearl Harbor attack.

I expected to be following the families soon. It would be terrible, but it was the expected course, and I would have my family and my community around me.

Yet increasingly, I felt I just couldn't do it. I had a gut feeling that it was just not right. What was happening was a violation of basic principles that the country stood for and that I had learned to believe deeply. Without accusation or trial 120,000 people—two-thirds of them US citizens—were to be deprived of their freedom, their possessions, and their livelihoods—just on the basis of their race.

I could not go along with it. I would lose my own self-respect if I did. I believed it was more realistic in the larger sense, more in keeping with the larger reality—to hold to the ideals that were set forth so clearly in the constitution.

My mother complimented me on my reasoning but cried as she pleaded with me to go with them. Their generation had always met discrimination and other difficulties with the belief that "The nail that sticks up is the one that gets hit." Better to adapt, to fit in, to follow the common pattern, the orders of authorities—not to make oneself conspicuous. But they had also taught me to stick to what I believed was right.

I knew one other person who believed as I did, but he finally yielded to his family's pleas and went with them. So in the end, I was absolutely alone in the stand I took. I took it because I had to. I wrote a statement explaining my position and turned myself in to the FBI the day after I was supposed to have reported for the "evacuation."

What Happened Next

Gordon was promptly put in the county jail. The northwest captain of the uprooting process was embarrassed to have this hold-out. The California captain had had 100% success with the program there, and this one wanted 100% too. He argued with Gordon and offered him early release to continue his education. When that didn't work, he threatened a long prison term.

Gordon recognized the captain's predicament and felt sorry for him. "You could drive me to the detention camp and just put me inside, behind the barbed wire," he suggested. "Then you'd have your 100%."

The captain shook his head. "No, that would be illegal."

Gordon was flabbergasted. The captain thought the whole uprooting was OK, but physically putting one unregistered person behind the barbed wire would be illegal!

When Gordon's case finally came to trial, the judge took the position that the military proclamations were the law. The constitution said that martial law could be proclaimed in a military emergency, and then that would be the law. But martial law had not been declared here, so Gordon knew that the constitution should still be followed.

Nevertheless, after hearing Gordon's arguments, the judge told the jury to disregard all the talk about the constitution and just decide if Gordon had violated the curfew and the evacuation order. Of course they agreed that he had, so the verdict was "guilty."

Gordon expected that higher courts would overturn his conviction, but he found that even the Supreme Court "had gone to war also." It upheld the guilty verdict. So Gordon served his sentence and then was put in one of the detention camps.

Since the War

After the war Gordon returned to college and got his PhD degree. He taught sociology, first in Lebanon and Egypt and then for many years at the University of Alberta. Through all those years and since his retirement, he has been concerned about minority rights and social justice and has worked hard to help Native-Americans and Asian Americans in Canada and the United States. He serves on Quaker committees in both countries, and four universities have awarded him honorary degrees.

But he always hoped that sometime the court decision against him might be overturned. Finally, more than forty years after the war, a lawyer named Peter Irons discovered that important evidence had been withheld at Gordon's earlier trial. A navy report that no incident of sabotage by Japanese-Americans

Gordon with his mother and one of his twin daughters after the war (1946).

had occurred was withheld, and a critical document had been changed for the hearing to make the "evidence" appear less racist.

Actually, by that time, the whole law that permitted the relocation of the Japanese had been rescinded. The Supreme Court said it was unconstitutional, as Gordon had claimed all along. And a special commission had agreed that the internment was not justified by military necessity but had resulted from "race prejudice, war hysteria, and a failure of political leadership."

Finally, in 1987, the charges against Gordon were overturned. Furthermore, the congress passed a law to give $20,000 to each Japanese-American victim of the relocation who was still living. It didn't begin to make up for the humiliation and financial losses they had suffered or for the three-year interruption in their lives, but the government was admitting that it had made a terrible mistake. It was reaffirming its belief in the principles stated so clearly in the constitution—that no one should be deprived of life or liberty on the basis of race and that any government action against a person should follow legal procedures.

More about Gordon Hirabayashi

Gordon would like us to know more about his early life and what helped make him the person he became. He writes:

My father came to the United States when he was nineteen and my mother came seven years later. They were married here but their marriage was arranged in Japan by their families. My father operated a small fruit and vegetable store in a farming community south of Seattle. I was the oldest of five children.

My parents had grown up in Buddhist homes but before they came to this country they had both become members of a small nondenominational Christian movement that had beliefs and values much like those of Quakers, with a strong emphasis on pacifism. Like the Friends, they had no pastor but shared in the responsibilities for spiritual nurture and growth. So when I found the Quakers later, I felt they stood for the same values that I did.

My parents did not allow Sunday sports or work except during emergencies like harvest time. Their lives emphasized the oneness of belief and behavior—doing all week what you say you believe on Sunday—as essential for integrity. For example, although I saw many farmers pack boxes of lettuce with the best-looking heads on top, my father would not do that because it would be a dishonest sample of what was in the whole crate. Seeing my parents consistently live their principles in the family, the neighborhood, and business taught me in ways that run deep, deeper than just words could have done.

While I was a child, and through my teenage period, I often felt that our religious group was too rigid and restrictive. I also had to cope with the conflicts between Japanese and Western ideals and values. Growing up in a Japanese home created serious problems at school. The teacher would encourage me by saying, "Speak up, Gordon! What do you think about that? Let's hear your view." The Japanese value system told me not to blurt out anything that was only half-baked. That would bring shame to me and my family. So I frequently sat like a sphinx in school and said nothing. But I took part in school activities and in Boy Scouts and even became a senior patrol leader.

When I entered the University of Washington after high school, I became active in the YMCA and began to learn about social action for more fairness and about opposing both war and preparation for war. I learned about conscientious objectors (COs), applied to be one, and was accepted. In fact, I was assigned to a camp for conscientious objectors and my friends had a farewell party for me, but just then the United States entered the war, and I was told that I couldn't go to the conscientious objectors' camp because people of Japanese ancestry weren't even eligible for being drafted.

Deciding not to obey the evacuation order was very hard for me. I had expected to go, but when the time came I realized I just couldn't do it. I believe that in a crisis, especially when you don't have all the facts and time is short, you have to trust your gut feelings. They represent the "bottom line" of all the experiences you've been sifting and making judgments about all through your life. They are your deepest, most dependable reality. Doing what your gut feeling tells you is right, whatever the consequences, is an essential aspect of your integrity.

Today I find it sensible to say: Live your principles. Live what you claim to believe—Sunday, every day, wherever you are. If love is a valid principle for home and community relations, so should it be for state and national principles. You build trust in others and self-respect in yourself by consistently practicing integrity.

When the charges against me were finally overturned in 1987, I was asked if I felt like celebrating after the constitution had failed me for so long. I said I felt it was never the constitution that had failed me but only people who were supposed to uphold it.

Going Deeper

Questions to Ponder

1. How does Gordon's life speak to you?
2. How do you feel about Gordon's disobeying the curfew and evacuation orders?
3. We value honesty and helping and caring for one another within our families and communities. Are we ever justified in trying to hurt people in our country or in other countries or undermine their safety?
4. What orders might you be willing to disobey?

Activities

1. Role play a conversation between Gordon and his mother and father, with Gordon telling them why he is disobeying the order and his parents saying why they think it is patriotic for them to go.
2. Find out how the Japanese people were treated in the internment camps.

3. How was the treatment of Japanese people and Japanese Americans during World War II the same and different from the treatment of immigrants from the Middle East since the Patriot Act became law?
4. Find out what constitutional rights the Patriot Act and subsequent legislation or decrees have taken away.
5. Work the crostic puzzle on pages 38–39. Answers on page 168.

Illustration Credits

Page 29: photograph courtesy of *Friends Journal*.

Page 30: photograph courtesy of *Seattle Post-Intelligencer* Collection, Museum of History and Industry.

Page 31: photograph courtesy of *Seattle Post-Intelligencer* Collection, Museum of History and Industry.

Page 34: photograph courtesy of Gordon Hirabayashi.

Page 39: puzzle provided courtesy of Amy Parrish

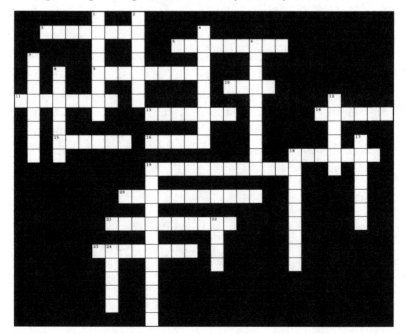

Crostic Puzzle

Across

3. to make people leave their homes
5. to prejudice
9. embarrass
10. to follow orders
11. people of Japan
13. to find guilty (hint: unscramble TICVONC)
14. another word for Friend
15. a large Egyptian stone monument with the body of a lion and the head of a man
16. not a citizen of the country
18. not legal
19. required enrollment into the military (hint: unscramble RIPSNOCNITCO)
20. very noticeable (hint: unscramble CUPCUSIONOS)
21. two words that mean military rules instead of the local government (hint: the first word describes what karate is _____ arts)
23. to destroy on purpose (hint: unscramble GASOBEAT)

Down

1. a person who follows the religious teachings of Buddha
2. the decision of a jury
4. to hold in custody; also a school punishment
6. confinement of people during war (hint: unscramble TENTMEN-RIN)
7. to see things as they should be (hint: unscramble LEASIDIM)
8. to see things as they are
12. time to be off the streets
17. one who loves his/her own country
18. sincerity, honesty
19. in the United States the Bill of Rights is a part of this document
22. abbreviation for American Friends Service Committee
24. to adjust or accommodate

Fay Honey Knopp
Lighting Dark Corners

by Liz Yeats

"The life of Fay Honey Knopp was proof of how one woman's belief in the power of good can bring light even to the darkest corners of our world." That's what the local newspaper in Rutland, Vermont, said about Honey Knopp in 1995 when she died. That's high praise for a Quaker and a very accurate description of the life and work of this spirited, positive, petite woman.

Little in Honey's childhood hinted that she would become that kind of person. She was born in Bridgeport, Connecticut, in 1918, just after World War I. Her father was a doctor. Her mother, like many in her generation, took care of the children and the home. The family had a Jewish heritage, but when Honey was growing up, they did not practice any religion.

Her family's values became evident during the Great

Honey's warmth was contagious.

Depression of the 1930s. Many families were without jobs and had little money for basic needs, including medical care.

Honey's father was one of the doctors in town who willingly treated patients even if they couldn't pay or could pay only with a chicken or a sack of potatoes.

Since times were hard, Honey had to stop school at seventeen and go to work to help support the family. Although she could have gotten scholarships, her request for education beyond high school was not honored by her parents, partly because they needed her income and partly, perhaps, because she was a woman. Instead, she moved to New York City and began working in a department store. She started with a low-level job but was soon promoted. By the age of twenty-one she was a successful buyer, someone who made decisions about what people would want to buy and selected the merchandise for the store.

Living in New York City, she met many interesting people, including her husband-to-be, Bert Knopp. Although most of her earnings went to her family, she saved enough to take a trip to Cuba. On that trip her eyes were opened to suffering and injustice she had never seen before or even imagined.

On the ship to Cuba she met a young graduate student who persuaded her to help him with his research into the condition of Cubans under Batista, who was the dictator of that island nation at the time. Honey met and talked with people who lived in shacks and never knew if they would have enough food for the next meal. There were few jobs, and even people who were working earned barely enough to survive. At the same time, there were very rich people in Cuba who owned beautiful homes and had many servants. She was struck by the great disparity in living conditions between the very rich and the very poor. It was much greater than she had grown up with in Bridgeport or than she was aware existed in the United States.

Honey also became aware of the dilemma faced by a group of German Jews she met on the boat to Cuba. She found their situation very troubling. The Holocaust was about to start in Germany, and the Jews were trying to escape, but the United States had refused to let them in. They had searched in Europe and the Western Hemisphere without finding any country that would admit them. They were probably going to have to return to Germany.

This upset Honey greatly. Her country, the United States, had always promised welcome to immigrants, especially those fleeing religious persecution, but these people had been denied entry. Honey always remembered those Jewish people wandering on a ship in the Atlantic and wondered what happened to them.

At the time, Honey didn't know what she could do to help either the Cubans or the Jews. She decided she needed to find out more about the world and its people. She knew she wanted to get involved in helping people find fairness and be able to meet their basic needs. Never again would she be blind to the victimization of helpless people. For the rest of her life she would stand up not only for her own rights but also for the rights of others.

Honey's early efforts were in progressive electoral politics, supporting candidates like Henry Wallace, who ran for president in 1948 promising to fight for the workingman. Doing this work, she met young people traveling the country in Quaker Peace Caravans, speaking and organizing for nuclear disarmament. They were talking about the horrific damage that nuclear bombs had done to the people of Hiroshima and Nagasaki, Japan. Honey listened carefully to their message that peace could not be secured through amassing weapons, but only through resolving conflicts nonviolently.

Honey had met Quakers before, as early as 1939 at a peace demonstration. She admired their courage in trying to bring the truth out where people could see it.

She found truth for herself in what they were saying and integrity in the way they were saying it. She began to work with others in her area to bring about disarmament.

In the 1950s, Bert and Honey married and soon had two children, a girl and a boy. They moved to a suburban area in Westport, Connecticut. As a young mother, Honey opened her home to the "Hiroshima maidens," young women who had been injured in the nuclear blasts in Japan at the end of World War II. They had come to the United States to get medical care and to share their experiences.[1]

Honey invited neighbors and friends to her house to meet and talk with these young women. Many who came were amazed at what they heard about the tremendous destruction and the continuing health problems in Japan that had been caused by the two atomic bombs that the United States had dropped. Honey knew that many people would have to be convinced that nuclear weapons were wrong before US policy could be changed. This was just the beginning of work toward that change.

Through the 1950s and early 1960s, Honey continued these activities. Sometimes they made her unpopular with her neighbors, and at times they upset Bert's business partners. But Bert always supported Honey. As a couple, they had deep love and respect for one another that grew over the years and provided a secure foundation from which Honey could risk following her leadings to do work for social change.

In the late 1950s, Honey joined others who were working for racial integration in Westport and continued to develop her skills in nonviolence through her activities in the civil rights movement that was gaining strength. A few years later, she was asked to go to Mississippi to travel with a mixed-race group of women and talk to southern white women who were just beginning to understand the problems that segregation was causing for everyone. She was a skillful leader on this trip, as shown in the following story.

---

[1] The story on page 74, about Barbara Reynolds, tells more about how their message was often misunderstood.

One night in rural Mississippi, Honey was driving in a car with several other women, both white and black. They became aware of a car following close behind them. They knew that earlier that summer three young civil rights workers from the north, two white and one black, had been driving on just such a road when they disappeared. Later they had been found dead.

There was certainly reason for the women to worry, and as the car continued to follow, some of them began to become upset. Honey stayed calm and slowed her vehicle allowing the other car to pull alongside. Then she leaned out the window and asked, "Are you lost? Can I help you find your way?" The men in the other car just stared and then drove away. We will never know what those men had intended for that interracial group of women. Maybe they meant no harm at all, or maybe they had meant to threaten the women with violence. But Honey's offer of help disarmed them in a nonviolent way, and the women arrived at their destination unharmed.

Those who knew Honey said she seemed almost oblivious to differences of race, ethnic background, and status. She just cared about people. She was a tiny woman with a big smile and seemingly boundless positive energy. A good listener, she embodied the principles of Quaker peacemaking in her interactions with everyone she met. Ever since her association with the peace caravaners, she had known that she had found a spiritual home, but like many convinced Friends, she waited for some time before becoming a member. She joined the Religious Society of Friends in 1962 and was later designated a "minister of record" to serve as a prison visitor. When this happened, she was one of only two people who had ever been permitted by the Federal Bureau of Prisons to visit every federal prison in the United States.

I met Honey soon after she became involved with prison visiting and prison problems during the Vietnam War. At that time all men between eighteen and twenty-six were subject to being drafted into the army. Most Quaker men and many others were applying to be recognized as conscientious objectors (COs), testifying before their draft boards that they were opposed to all wars for religious and moral reasons. Some of these men were granted CO status and did alternative service in mental hospitals, schools, or other nonprofit organizations. Some of those who were denied CO status refused to go into the army and were arrested and put in a federal prison for a year or two, as were some who even refused to do alternative service because they believed that would still help the war effort. They didn't want to cooperate with the draft law at all. These men were often called draft resisters.

Honey was active in opposing the Vietnam War in many ways, including counseling men who were applying to be COs, helping them to clarify their thoughts and feelings about opposition to war. Over a six-year period she was a volunteer director of several programs for the American Friends Service Committee, including its Nonviolent Action/ Training Program in Peace Education.

Honey also decided that the least she could do to support the draft resisters and their families would be to visit them in prison as often as her busy schedule allowed. Visiting prisons awakened her to a concern that large numbers of prisoners were serving long sentences during which they often lived in difficult conditions and had no chance for education that would change their violent behavior or prepare them for constructive lives when their jail terms were over. She especially became concerned about the men and women who had been jailed because of sex offenses. As she visited and listened to them tell their stories, she recognized that just locking these people up and not providing therapy to help them change was futile and wasteful. Ultimately released, many continued the same behaviors for which they had been put in prison.

In 1964, Honey founded the Prison Research Education Action Program (PREAP), which began research on how these people could be helped. By 1975, she was sure there needed to be a book that would urge the need to change prisons and ultimately abolish them. Lacking the ability to pay salaries to a group of researchers and writers and having a life-long interest in empowering young people, she invited a group of young adults to live in her house, with Bert and herself, for the whole year it took to create that book. Titled *Instead of Prisons: A Handbook for Abolitionists*, the book was published in 1976. It was one of the first to help many people understand and become active in changing the lives of both prisoners and their victims.

During this period, Honey and the Reverend Robert Horton also established Prisoner Visitation and Support (PVS). This agency trains and certifies people, Quakers and others, who then visit in Federal prisons on a regular basis. They may visit only one person or several over the years. Visitors listen to prisoners, help them identify and meet their needs for therapy and education, and sometimes provide spiritual support. This group still works in federal prisons today.

Many of these prison visitors have gone on, like Honey, to become involved with other programs in the prisons, such as the Alternatives to Violence Program. This is a program that conducts intensive weekend workshops in prisons, teaching prisoners to deal with anger and conflicts without violence.

In the 1980s, Honey and Bert moved to Vermont, where their involvement with prisons evolved into yet another organization to work with offenders and victims, the Safer Society Program and Press. Under Honey's leadership, it grew to be an internationally respected program dedicated to research and advocacy for crime prevention, with special emphasis on treatment for sex offenders. Honey won many honors and awards over the years and had many chances to speak to groups about what she was doing and what she had learned. Almost up until her death in August of 1995, Honey was able to carry out research on offenders and their victims. A major result of this research has been the publication and distribution of many books and

Honey as spokesperson for good causes.

materials for children and adults and both victims and offenders, on how to prevent sexual crimes.

The last time I saw Honey she was standing under a tree on a hill in Vermont. Her eyes were smiling and sparkling from under a big floppy hat as she engaged someone in a story about how even sexual offenders can change and become part of the healing process for themselves and their victims. There was Honey, affirming her Quaker belief in "that of God in everyone" and working to heal the world by working for the basic rights of others, no matter who they were or what they had done.

After she died, one of the prisoners she had visited regularly wrote from a jail in California, "She was family and friend to all of us who felt we were lost somewhere in time from making incorrect choices. Honey's spirit will live on forever in our hearts."

Going Deeper

Questions to Ponder

1. How does Honey's life speak to you?
2. Do nations obey the same moral principles as individuals? Why or why not?

3. Do you think our society could manage without prisons? What might work instead?
4. How did working with Friends effect Honey's life?

Activities

1. Make up a story with a different ending based on Honey's experience driving black and white women together in the rural south (p. 44).
2. List the names of the organizations Honey worked with or founded. What kind of personal characteristics are needed for this type of work?
3. Consider a class project that would involve working with people in prison.

Illustration Credits

Page 40: photograph courtesy of *Friends Journal.*
Page 47: photograph courtesy of New England Yearly Meeting.

Bill Kreidler
Win-Win Solutions

by Liz Yeats

B ill Kreidler was totally alive. He taught, he wrote books, and he even did a bit of tap dancing on the side. His life spoke loudly—to young and to old, to Friends and to non-Friends, and especially to children. He might be playing a game with his young friends one moment and discussing Catholic mystics or prayer with some older friends the next. Bill taught from his heart, from his experience, and through his stories—all of it with a great deal of humor and love.

For many years of his life Bill taught elementary school. He told me the story about how he decided to become a teacher. In high school, he loved acting and was involved with drama classes and performances, but he knew he didn't want to become an actor. Although his mother was a teacher, he hadn't thought about teaching until one day an "angel" arrived in his life.

At the time, he had a job as a "soda jerk," as it was called, serving ice cream and sodas behind the counter at a Howard

Johnson's Restaurant. One day a new person was hired and the manager asked Bill to train him. Bill was showing the new fellow how to do the work when a complete stranger, who was sitting at the counter and had been watching, said, "You know you would make a good teacher. You do it so naturally." That was Bill's first experience of an "angel." Several times later, "angels" would appear in his life.

Somehow, Bill knew now that becoming a teacher was right for him. And when Bill decided something, he would move ahead to do it, "as way opened."

Bill had grown up in a small, close, loving farm community in upstate New York among rolling hills of farmland, mostly dairy farms. He had gone to the elementary school where his mother taught, and he had spent much of his free time playing and working outdoors. Bill didn't grow up a Quaker but went to the Dutch Reformed Church. There he learned that many of his relatives in Holland had suffered a great deal during World War II, had helped Jews by hiding them, and had lived through years of hunger and lack of material goods with great courage. Those stories of courage helped Bill know that he wanted to be like those people. He wanted to do something in his life that would help others.

Life did not always come easily for Bill, however. Growing up, he always felt different. He wasn't interested in sports and he had a hard time making friends. His family was supportive though, and he did all right until high school when they moved to a more populated area outside the city of Albany. The new school was much larger. Bill became unhappy and had few friends.

Not one just to let himself be sad, he made a plan. He saved all the money he could, and just after Christmas he got on a bus and went to New York City. There he got a room at the YMCA and began thinking about looking for a job. He kept safe and busy, going to museums and plays and trying not to think about the future or how his actions might be affecting his family.

Naturally, his parents were frantic. They couldn't imagine where he had gone and they called the police. For five days they hunted for him. Finally, they found him. It was a relief for everyone. Down deep, Bill knew that running away would not solve anything. He just didn't know how to tell his parents how unhappy he was. Now they knew, and he could come home and go back to school knowing that everyone wanted to help him. He developed his interest in drama, got that job as a soda jerk, and studied hard to get into college.

In high school, one of the things that made Bill feel different was that he knew early that he was gay. This was difficult for him, not because he felt bad about being gay but because he grew up in a time when no one talked about homosexuality.

He always seemed to know that God loved him just as he was and that gave him comfort. However, since he couldn't talk to anyone about it, he didn't have anyone with whom to share his feelings. That made him feel alone. He didn't know anyone else who was gay, and he wondered what it felt like to other gay people.

After high school, Bill went to college to become a teacher. After he graduated, he went to Boston to look for a job. He found there were already too many teachers in Boston. The only jobs available were in some tough schools where teaching would be very difficult. He took one of those jobs and soon found himself struggling just to keep the students in his class from being disruptive. No one could learn what he was trying to teach. He decided he would have to start by teaching them better ways of getting along with one another. That's what led him to trying to help his students resolve the conflicts that they kept getting into. As he experimented and found ways that worked, he developed more.

He decided to go back to school for a master's degree. For his final paper he collected successful exercises that he had worked out for resolving conflict and wrote about them. One day when he was meeting with his advisor, the advisor said, "Why don't you publish this as a book so you can share what you have learned?" Here was another "angel," pointing Bill to what he should do next.

Bill became a writer. He did publish that first collection of conflict resolution exercises, and many teachers used it. That led him to write several more books. Some were for helping older or younger children. In the process, he decided to stop classroom teaching and go to work for Educators for Social Responsibility, a group of teachers who train other teachers and write curriculum for other teachers to use. Bill wrote several books for them and trained teachers all over this country and in other parts of the world in the techniques he had developed.

These were happy times for Bill. He had found he could give people help they really needed. Another reason it was a happy time for him was that people had begun talking about sexual orientation and he was able to become part of a whole community of gay and lesbian people. He wrote for a gay and lesbian newspaper in Boston and began to make contacts in the Quaker community. Soon he knew

many gay and lesbian Quakers. He became part of a faith community that celebrated and acknowledged his true self, and he was able to help other people deal with issues about sexual orientation in his local meeting, his yearly meeting, and beyond.

Bill's hardest challenges were yet to come. When he was in his thirties, he learned that he was infected with HIV. That was a time when doctors knew very little about the disease. One thing they knew for certain: Bill would die sooner than might have been expected otherwise. Bill did two things after that. He took care of himself and he doubled up on the things he was doing in his life. It was a hard balance.

One new thing he decided to do was find out more about how other people dealt with such difficult times. This led him to a study of Catholic mystic saints such as Teresa of Avila and Julian of Norwich. And what Bill learned, Bill taught. He shared his experience with others without holding anything back. He found that made him go deeper in recognizing unknown parts of himself. He felt he became more of a whole person. Toward the end of his life, he was concentrating on forgiveness.

Bill died on June 10, 2000. I spoke to him for the last time two months before. He still had lots of plans for books and workshops. At the end, he had very little energy left, but he still enjoyed telling a good story. He died with a loving community around him who mourn and miss him. It's sad that he died so young, so full of life, and with so much still to teach. The life he lived was a very full one that gave many other people skills for living loving and creative lives. In this author's opinion Bill Kreidler was a true "Quaker saint."

Going Deeper

Questions to Ponder

1. How does Bill's life speak to you?
2. What organized programs exist in your school for helping you deal with conflicts constructively?
3. Have you had any hunches about what you want your life work to be?
4. What is a win-win solution? Describe one from this chapter.

Activities:

1. Look up one of Bill Kreidler's books and, in pairs, arrange to try out one or two of the exercises.
2. Make up a story about running away from home.
3. Research conflict resolution resources for your class and school.

Illustration Credits

Page 49: photograph by John Meyers.
Pages 50–51: photographs by Joanne Clapp Fullagar.
Page 53: photograph by Joanne Clapp Fullagar.

Sigrid Lund
Daring to Say "No"

by Marnie Clark

Sigrid Lund, a Norwegian Quaker, was born Sigrid Helliesen. She didn't start out as a Quaker, though. Like her family and all her friends, she was baptized as a baby in the Norwegian State Church. She was expected to confirm her baptism in that church at the age of sixteen. Confirmation meant accepting the teachings of the church and becoming a full member.

But when Sigrid reached 16, she realized she couldn't do that. She said later, "I knew I could not confirm that baptism by accepting the Church's teaching on salvation through baptism. The whole concept of some people being saved and others being condemned was completely against my belief in a God of love. Neither could I accept that it was right for any person to take over the guilt of another."[1]

1 Margaret Gibbins, *Sigrid Lund: Portrait of a Norwegian* Friend, London: Quaker Home Service and Near East Section of Friends World Committee for Consultation, 1982, p. 1.

Refusing confirmation was unheard of. All her friends were going to be confirmed. Sigrid's mother did not try to change her mind but insisted that Sigrid go to the five-month preparatory classes with all the other 16-year-olds so she would be very sure she knew what she was rejecting.

Sigrid did that, and at the end she had a long talk with her pastor. To her surprise, he agreed that it would not be right for her to be confirmed because it would be dishonest. He asked her if she had ever heard of the Quakers. She replied "Yes, but only in history books—a peculiar kind of people." Her pastor said, "Well, I am sure you will hear more about them in the future." He was right, but not right away.

Early Years

Sigrid was the youngest of four children in a close, loving family. Her Swedish mother was deeply religious, a liberal thinker, warmhearted, artistic, and keenly interested in her children's activities. Her father, a busy lawyer, was an active supporter of the National Theater of Oslo.

Sigrid, two and a half years old.

Sigrid had a beautiful voice and took training in Oslo, Copenhagen, and Paris to be a concert singer. She gave several concerts, but her singing career ended when she developed health problems. By that time she had a husband, Diderich Lund, and a baby boy, Bernt, a bright, happy, attractive child. A few years later, their second baby, Erik, turned out to be mentally handicapped. Erik was so loving and trust-ing that Sigrid developed a deep love for him and even learned to be patient—something new for her.

Helping Jewish Refugees

In the 1930s, Hitler and the Nazis came to power in Germany. Hitler encouraged the Germans to believe that they were a master race who were destined to control Europe for the next thousand years. He told them other races were infe-rior, especially the Jews, whom he blamed for many of Germany's economic problems. At first, he let Jews leave Germany and thousands did so. Later, Jews were rounded up and deported to concentration camps where most were killed.

When Jewish refugees began to arrive in Norway, Sigrid worked with groups who were helping them. After World War II broke out, she was asked to go to Czechoslovakia to bring a group of forty Jewish children to the safety of foster homes in Norway. It was a hard trip. She saw little children being treated with harshness and hatred just because they were Jewish, but she got them safely to Norway and found homes for them all.

No one had dreamed that Germany would invade Norway. But one April morning the world woke up to find that it had happened. Suddenly the Nazis controlled all of Norway. Sigrid quickly burned all the papers related to the peace organizations she had been working in so the Nazis would not find any of the names and addresses of people who had been helping the refugees.

Two cities in the west of Norway had been destroyed by the Germans, and Sigrid was asked to lead a group taking truckloads of supplies to the people there. She got the neces-sary permits for safe passage, but on the way the trucks were stopped. German officers demanded to speak with the leader.

A woman? The leader wouldn't believe it. He ordered the group to turn back. Quietly, Sigrid persuaded the officers to let them go ahead, and they did.

Underground Resistance

An underground resistance movement became organized almost at once, and Sigrid's family became involved in many of its activities. One of their biggest jobs was to help people who were in trouble with the Nazis. They would warn them, often hide them—in all kinds of places—and sometimes help them escape to Sweden.

One day she got word that children were to be taken the next day. That night she went to a children's home, and she and a woman doctor moved all the children, hidden under covers, to a safe place and later sent them all to Sweden. The Jewish children she had brought from Czechoslovakia earlier were scattered throughout Norway. Even so, she found and saved all but three of them.

Although listening to radios was forbidden by the Nazis, Sigrid's teenage son Bernt listened to British broadcasts every night. He and his friends would write a news sheet and distribute it during the night. Norwegian citizens had no other way of knowing what was really happening in the world and in the war. Eventually, the Nazis found the boys and sent Bernt to a concentration camp in Germany. Sigrid was afraid she would never see him again.

By this time, Sigrid's husband was in Sweden working for the Norwegian Government in Exile, and her other son, Eric, was living with friends in another part of Norway. Then one night Sigrid herself became a refugee. When she was warned that the Nazis were looking for her, she left with several others, hidden under a tarp in a truck. A few hours later, they walked through woods to Sweden.

Sigrid As a Refugee

A British Quaker visiting Norway had been staying with the Lund family when the Nazis came. She escaped with Sigrid, and in Sweden she introduced Sigrid to her Quaker friends there, many of whom became Sigrid's and Diderich's close friends too. About this time the Germans started releasing Scandinavian prisoners and sending them to Sweden. The Quakers were helping them, and Sigrid began helping them too. Imagine her joy when one day one of the released prisoners turned out to be her own son Bernt.

Sigrid with the man who led her group to safety in Sweden during World War II, retracing that route in 1978.

Quakerism and Service after the War

When the war finally ended, the Lunds went back to Norway, and Sigrid became leader of a group of volunteer relief workers in parts of northern Norway that had been devastated in the war. Young Quakers from the American Friends Service Committee (AFSC) and the British Friends Ambulance Unit came to help.

Their British friend returned too and lived with them for another four years, during which they nurtured a tiny Quaker worship group. When it became a full Quaker meeting, Sigrid was the first of several attenders to become a member. She had come to believe that the Religious Society of Friends was where she belonged. Her pastor had been right all those years before.

Asked what it was that attracted her toward Quakerism, she said,

> I found there not a system of doctrines and rites . . . but a seeking attitude, a seeking to understand more fully the working of the divine force and to find one's right place and role in human relationships. . . . Another aspect of Quakerism that attracted me from the start was its breadth of vision, its tolerance toward people of other beliefs. It tolerates too within its own membership great diversities in theological matters, something which to me enriches it.[2]

In the years after the war, her life continued to speak of her passion for peace and service, though it was not as exciting or dangerous as it had been. When her husband went to India to administer a fisheries program helping fishermen build better boats and and use more efficient methods, she went along and helped a doctor in his work treating villagers with skin diseases. She enjoyed visiting villagers in their homes and made friends wherever she went.

Later she joined the Quaker team that was working at the brand new United Nations in New York and Sigrid hoped that the United Nations would make it possible for all the countries of the world, big and small, to live together in peace. She hoped it could help

Sigrid in a conference at the United Nations, as a representative of Friends World Committee for Consultation.

2 Margaret Gibbins, *Sigrid Lund: Portrait of a Norwegian* Friend, London: Quaker Home Service and Near East Section of Friends World Committee for Consultation, 1982, p. 14.

people learn to solve their problems in ways that would make things better for everybody.

Sigrid also became active in the Friends World Committee for Consultation (FWCC), which is a network of all the Quaker groups around the world. Only

Sigrid (right) in Kenya with her friend and biographer, Margaret Gibbons.

six years after the war it sent her to Germany to help people who had been enemies learn to respect and trust each other. When she got there, she found it was hard for her even to hear the German language because of her bitter memories of what Germans had done in Norway. But she believed that there was that of God in Germans too, and she found she was able to talk to them about friendship and understanding.

These meetings were hard for the Germans, too. At one meeting, an elderly man wondered how a woman from Norway could talk with them in a friendly way after the terrible things she had seen the Nazis do. He asked her to lead the group in praying the Lord's prayer in Norwegian while they would all say it in German. She was unable to reply for a moment, surely thinking of her family's experiences, then nodded her head and began in her clear, strong voice, "Fader Vaar. . . ." It was an emotional experience for all of them as they felt the presence of the same Spirit.

To Sigrid, Quakerism was not a set of beliefs but a way of life. She experienced God not as a personal being but as a spiritual force in her life. She saw Jesus as fully human. In fact, she said that if he had been part God, his life and teaching would not have meant so much to her because then she wouldn't have been able to see him as an example of the best that human life can be. She deeply believed that Jesus' message of love and caring applied to all situations and that all life is sacred. She also believed that other religions have much to teach us.

Sigrid's Quakerism only broadened and deepened the strong convictions and strength that she showed as a teenager when she refused to be confirmed in her state church. Her whole life showed that same courage. Sigrid died in 1987.

Going Deeper

Questions to Ponder

1. How does Sigrid's life speak to you?
2. What do you feel strongly enough about to refuse to do in the face of your friends' and family's contrary expectations?
3. Sigrid believed that love is the appropriate response to every situation. Can you think of any situation where a loving response would not be appropriate? If so, please explain.
4. Describe a situation where you "loved" your enemies. What did you do?

Activities

1. Find out about the Quaker United Nations Office (QUNO).
2. Invite someone who has worked in a resistance movement to come and tell you about it.
3. What other actions of nonviolent resistance occured in Norway and Denmark during the Nazi occupation?

Illustration Credits

Page 55: photograph courtesy of Ruthanna Hadley.
Page 56: photograph courtesy of Bernt Lund.
Pages 59–61: photographs courtesy of Bernt Lund.

Marlene and Steve Pedigo
Growing into Urban Ministry[1]

by Marlene Morrison Pedigo

My heart was pounding and I wondered if I would leave alive. What had started as a basketball scrimmage between two community teams in a youth center on Chicago's impoverished West Side had turned into a small riot.

At the beginning of the game, the bleachers had come alive with yelling, clapping, and hooting for each team. Although our team played hard, they were losing as the game progressed. In the closing minutes, one of our guards made an insulting remark to an opposing player. A fist fight erupted on the floor and spread to the other

Marlene and Steve and their three children, Joel, Nathan and Anna.

[1] This story—about Marlene's ministry with her husband, Steve, in Chicago, Illinois—is based primarily on Marlene Morrison Pedigo's book, *New Church in the City*, published in 1988 by Friends United Press, Richmond, Indiana.

team members. Soon it became a free-for-all, with even the spectators spilling onto the floor. My husband Steve attempted to separate two players and got a swift, hard left to the jaw.

I rose to my feet in the bleachers, but I was too stunned and frightened to move away. I could hear whistles blowing above the angry cries as adults shoved the youth out of the building. The youth center's director ran down the hall to telephone the police. Out team were locked in the gym for their protection. The mob outside pounded on the door and screamed threats.

When the police finally came and escorted us through the dark to our van, we found that the mob had smashed our lights, torn off the windshield wipers, and flattened all our tires.

This happened in 1980. We had moved to the Chicago area not long before. Unknowingly, in planning the game, we had crossed one of the invisible "turf" boundaries that are a harsh reality of Chicago's street gangs. We had learned the hard way.

My first impulse was to tell Steve that I was going back to my parents' farm in Iowa. Through our prayers and tears that night, however, we had an inner confirmation that this *was* where we were supposed to be. Steve had wanted to work with inner city youth since his own troubled childhood. He felt that he was making some headway with this new basketball team and the Wednesday night meetings at our home, which included some of the girls in the neighborhood. We had just gotten a taste of the violence that is an everyday part of the lives of our new young friends. More violence was to come in this explosive three-by-six-block area called Cabrini-Green, and we would have much more to learn.

The Cabrini Green Neighborhood

In the 1930s, 40s, and 50s, the low row houses near the Chicago River factory area, near downtown Chicago, were owned and operated by the Chicago Housing Authority

(CHA). They were rented mostly to middle-class and low-income Italian immigrants. The CHA took care of the grounds, had regular trash pick-ups, and supplied tools for home repair and gardening. With seeds given to them, the tenants were able to keep attractive gardens and lawns. There was a warm community atmosphere, with adults watching out for one another's children. People slept out in their yards on a hot summer's night, and they could leave their doors unlocked.

Things changed in the 1960s, when the city turned the operation of the area over to the tenants. At the same time the city built high-rise buildings around the neat little row homes. The population of that three-by-six-block area swelled from 8,755 to approximately 26,000, three-fourths of whom were under the age of 21. The city no longer supplied yard and home repair tools and plantings, and trash collections were reduced. Garbage piled up because the incinerator at the end of each block was fired up only twice a week. As the original Italian workers acquired enough money, they moved away. The residents who were left behind could not afford to buy their own equipment. Rent had been raised from $36 a month to $500.

By 1980, the area had become divided by gangs into areas with clear boundaries that people could not safely cross. The Cobra Stones, the Vice Lords, and the Black Gangster Disciples each had their own turf. The gangs recruited young people early, often by the age of eight or ten, a time when children are wanting to belong to a peer group. Instead of joining Boy Scouts or Campfire Girls, they became identified with a gang—a group that then dictated their lifestyle and future. Each gang's turf boundaries were openly marked with symbols on the corners of buildings. Their members identified themselves by a tilt of their hats, a variety of hand gestures, and the colors of their clothes.

Searching for My Life Purpose

This was the setting to which we had come. These children's lives were so different from those of my childhood! I grew up in rural Grinnell, Iowa. The realities of war, poverty, illiteracy, and crime were unknown in my daily existence. My family, like many families in our town, had been farmers for generations in the same township, ever since my ancestors had first purchased the deep, rich virgin soil from the state of Iowa. In the evening, I liked to walk in the quiet fields to a favorite "reflection spot." There were fresh fragrances and soft noises. I wondered at the greatness of God. In the peace that surrounded me, I prayed for answers to my inner unrest, seeking to know the purpose for which God had designed my life.

While I was in high school, a Quaker evangelist couple from Ireland, John and Dorothy Sinton, visited us for a week of nightly meetings. One evening Dorothy Sinton delivered one of the most memorable sermons of my life. A recorded Friends minister, Dorothy was in her late middle age. When she rose to speak, she did not raise her voice or pound on the pulpit. Instead, she opened her Bible to read Isaiah 29:13–16:

> The Lord says: These people come near me with their mouth and honor me with their lips, but their hearts are far from me. Their worship of me is made up only of rules taught by men. . . .
>
> Woe to those who go to great depths to hide their plans from the Lord,
>
> Who do their work in darkness and think, "Who sees us? Who will know? . . .
>
> Can the pot say of the potter, "He knows nothing?"

I came to see each of us as being like a lump of clay with tremendous potential, to realize that each of us can place ourselves in the hands of our Creator, as Master Potter, who will fashion us with great care into a vessel that can be used for

His service. That night, I openly committed myself to becoming whatever God would want me to be and to serving the Lord to the best of my ability. Little did I realize that evening that this decision would lead me into Cabrini-Green.

When I married Steve soon after we graduated from William Penn College in Iowa, God opened an unexpected door for urban ministry. Steve had vowed to work with youth since he was a teen, self-imprisoned in his bedroom to keep out the conflict and strife of his family. When he received the invitation to come to Chicago, he excitedly made the arrangements. I was hesitant. I was afraid of the unknown. I was a country girl. Would I be able to adjust to this radically different setting? Could God be calling me so soon to spread my wings and leave my safe environment behind?

I shared my heart's turmoil with a friend. She reassured me from her deep faith: "God never calls people without also equipping them for the ministry. You must trust God to do this as you step out in faith."

Starting Our Ministry

At first, I was just a bystander, watching Steve coach basketball games because I didn't want to sit home alone. After all, this was his dream, not mine. I prayed for guidance, for a way I could become more active. Then one night, as I gingerly walked into the noisy gymnasium, I noticed two teenage girls sitting by themselves. I sat down next to then and introduced myself. We cheered and shared the joy of victory together. Afterward, I invited the girls and some of the team members to our house for hot dogs and the card game "Pit." By the end of the evening, I had my answer from the Lord. Besides being a support for Steve and his ministry, I could have a definite ministry of my own to these girls. It took several months of meeting young people before we had our first formal meeting in our home.

One of the ways Steve got to know new teens was to help out in the athletic department of the local high school. Often he sat with them as they ate their hamburgers and French fries at the cafeteria tables. He came to be known fondly as the "Dud Man" for his habit of telling one-line jokes. To start a conversation, Steve would slip out from his pocket a piece of paper containing three jokes taken from his private library of joke books.

"Why was the Mama flea so upset?" he quizzed his munching audience.

Groans and laughter erupted as the students groped to guess the punch line first.

"Because her children were going to the dogs!"

Such conversations opened the way for more serious topics. Often they came up without warning, like the conversation about death when one of their camp counselors was hit by lightning on a camping trip. Life was full of surprises and challenges for us and the kids.

Broader Needs

A boy was killed by the police. What a horrible thing to happen! Worse yet, no one was doing anything about it. Young people die every year in our neighborhood. Some make the newspapers—some don't. Some who died had played ball with Steve's group or were in my after school program. We wanted to make a difference. The best way we could see to do that was through one person at a time.

We talked to a probation officer and were assigned a foster teen from an abusive home. This was an alternative to jail for him. We didn't even get out of the court house before he showered us with angry words. I wasn't so sure we had done the right thing. He stayed with us for four years, however, and we have kept in touch with him since. He's now 30. When his term was up, we became foster parents of several other teenage boys who were in trouble.

As a result of gang shootings around a local grammar school, the superintendent of schools wanted to close our neighborhood school and send our children to other schools. This would have put a great hardship on our community. Steve organized the churches and they came up with a "peace plan." Trained parents with walkie-talkies would protect small groups of children on their way to and from school. It would be supported by a local company and financed by the school. One of the ministers was hired to run the project. Later, other areas of Chicago used a similar plan. Again, however, it had taken the death of a child to bring about a positive solution to a problem.

Making Friends with the Neighbors

When we first moved to Chicago, we lived a little west of Cabrini-Green. After the neighbors saw young people of color coming and going from our house, someone set our garage on fire. In our attempt to cross racial barriers, we felt like aliens in our own country. The black community wondered what our ulterior motives might be for coming there to live. Our white immigrant neighbors worried that we might move Cabrini-Green blacks onto their block.

Shortly after our garage burned the second time, Steve and a volunteer were showered with dirt and rocks as they walked down the sidewalk to our home. Later that day, Steve sat on the front steps and waited for the boys who had done it to walk past again. As two of them approached, he said, "Hey, boys, why did you throw those rocks?"

Trying to ignore Steve, the boys ran to their house. One of them went inside, while the other lingered on the steps outside. Steve walked over to him.

"Hey, why did you throw those rocks?" Steve asked again, in a calm voice.

"'Cause you're bringin' blacks into the neighborhood," the boy answered toughly. "Well, I live here just like you do. I own a house here. Don't throw rocks again," was Steve's rejoinder.

Suddenly, one of the boys' mothers appeared in the doorway. "Are you going to move blacks into our neighborhood?" she asked.

"I'm not doing that," was his reply.

"Well, I thought you were," she said defensively.

"If you want to know something, why don't you ask me? It's hard to understand what is bothering people when they throw rocks. Next time, ask," Steve encouraged her.

"I will," was her response as she turned back into her home.

Shortly after, when she became ill, her son Ron asked Steve to take her to the hospital. Steve did so and also encouraged Ron to pursue his GED—his high school degree. Ron began to drop by our home to talk to Steve about what was happening in his life and to receive encouragement. God works in mysterious ways.

Starting a Quaker Meeting

For several years during our youth ministry at our home, we led Bible studies for the teenagers. Over the years, these sessions began to include more young adults. Slowly, the focus became one of worship. We moved the time to Sunday afternoons, still in our living room. We added music, then a choir. In our prayer times, we told about the Quaker practice of each person feeling free to express their inner hearts to God.

"Thank you, God, for waking me up this morning and giving me life."

"Dear Lord, please look after my mother. She is really going through a struggle right now. Help her to turn to you."

The spirit of God could be sensed in the earnestness of those who prayed. When we began talking about what it means to be a Quaker, I can still remember some of the first comments.

"I thought Quakers were the people who make oatmeal."

"Didn't Quakers live in the olden days? I thought they all died."

"Aren't Quakers the people who dress in black clothes and wear black hats?"

Their questions reflected how little many people today understand the beliefs of the Religious Society of Friends. We had to start from the beginning.

Over time, in addition to Steve's basketball team, we started a day care program and a summer camp. We also have an after school program for thirty children. In 1983, the Catholic Diocese gave us an old, vacant school building. I asked them for an additional $5,000 to help repair it, which they gave us. In 1986, we started a Friends meeting in that building. Today both young people and their parents attend it.

I entered this experience with my feet dragging, coming to Chicago only because Steve felt he had a call. I did not feel equipped at all. In time, my love and concern for the people I was meeting helped me overcome my fears.

I didn't know it at the time, but to some extent Steve was having the same experience. He says,

> I was very conscious of being white, and I was fearful because of all the rumors I'd heard about violence. Also, I didn't play ball very well then, and I didn't know the customs of the playground or how to pick up teams. I made a lot of mistakes and would leave the playground feeling like a fool.
>
> What I learned was that the playground action is like a courtroom. The arguments and yelling are, in fact, just the way they work. Where I came from, yelling and arguing were a prelude to a fight. Here, it is just part of the game, and the one who argues in the most logical manner wins. In fact, if the

arguing on these playgrounds leads to fighting, it is seen as a sign of weakness. I had a lot to learn. It is intimidating to enter a different culture. Hanging in there is the most important thing.

And hanging in there is what Steve and Marlene have done. Their goal has been to change lives, one by one. They believe there is a great need for Quakers to live Christ's peace in the midst of urban violence—to stand with those who are too often overlooked in society.

Going Deeper

Questions to Ponder

1. How do Marlene and Steve's lives speak to you?
2. If you were teaching young people about Quakerism, what would you tell them?
3. When you meet someone from another culture who seems to see things differently or do things that puzzle you, what do you do?
4. Have you ever had a "reflection place" the way Marlene did as a child? Describe it. Do you have one now? Why or why not?

Activities

1. For over 300 years, Quaker women have been active in various kinds of ministry. Marlene mentions three of these women in her book, *New Church in the City*: Margaret Fell, Elizabeth Fry, and Mary Dyer. Find out about and discuss what kinds of ministry each of them did.
2. Look up the verse from Isaiah 29:13–16 and tell in your own words what it means. Look up the same verse in a different translation of the Bible and compare the wording. How are they the same or different?

3. What does it mean to be a recorded minister in the Quaker tradition? How does a person become one? Who do you know who is or might become a recorded minister?

Illustration Credits

Page 63: photograph courtesy of Marlene Pedigo.

Barbara Reynolds
Friend of the Hibakusha

by Beth Parrish

As a young girl, Barbara was entranced by *The Japanese Twins*, a storybook about children's life in Japan by Lucy Fitch Perkins. From it she learned to love Japanese customs. She and her friends spent hours pretending to be the characters in that book. They removed their shoes when they entered the house, drank tea, and pretended to sleep on mats on the floor. Little did she know how important Japan would be in her grown-up life.

Her first chance to live in Japan came many years later in 1951, after World War II. By then she had married and changed her name from Leonard to Reynolds. Her husband was sent to Hiroshima to study the effects of the US nuclear bomb on Japanese children who had survived. The United States had dropped a nuclear bomb on that city

Barbara as a child.

near the end of the war. Thousands of people had been killed and many survivors were still suffering from radiation sickness.

Barbara and Earle and their three children lived on the military base there for three years. Earle's research showed that the closer children had been to the explosion, the longer they took to mature, and the more severely stunted their eventual growth was. Also, the leukemia rate in Hiroshima was ten times the national Japanese average. Through further research, he learned that radiation causes both stillbirths and abnormal births, from harelips or birthmarks to more serious problems, such as cataracts, cerebral palsy, bone cancer, and leukemia.

The Phoenix

While they were in Hiroshima, Earle supervised the building of a two-masted sailing boat. It was 50 feet long and had a cabin where the family would be able to live on long trips. They named the boat *Phoenix of Hiroshima* after the Greek myth of a bird that rose to life from its own ashes. That was what the destroyed city of Hiroshima was doing while they were living there.

The *Phoenix*.

When his work was finished, Earle was eager to sail around the world in the *Phoenix*. Barbara was not at all eager to do that. She was afraid of the sea, perhaps because her father had drowned in a sailing accident. And what about school for the children?

Barbara finally agreed to sail as far as Hawaii, where their older child, Tim, would get a plane back to school in the United States. By the time they reached Hawaii, she had a change of heart, and Barbara, Earle, and their daughter Jessica did sail the *Phoenix* all the way around the world, with many brief stops along the way.

It turned out to be a wonderful adventure. Without schoolmates, jobs, and conveniences, they learned to work together for the safety of the *Phoenix* and learned more about one anothers' special gifts. In ports where they stopped, they learned about different cultures and answered questions about their experiences in Japan. They were gone four years.

The Golden Rule

Back in Hawaii, they began another adventure, one for which they were well prepared because of their time in Japan. In Honolulu, capital of Hawaii, they met four people from the United States who had arrived on a sailboat, the *Golden Rule*. They were Quakers who had heard that the United States was going to test nuclear bombs over the Pacific Ocean near islands southwest of Hawaii. They had realized that the testing meant the United States was still preparing for the possibility of some day using nuclear bombs again in another war.

These Quakers and many others believed that the nuclear bombing in Japan had been immoral because of the massive destruction and many deaths it had caused and also because of the long-lasting effects of radiation which could cause genetic damage for many generations. They believed that our country should never use nuclear weapons again and should not be preparing for the possibility by improving its nuclear capability. They knew that even the bomb testing was dangerous because it would release dangerous radioactivity that could drift all around the world.

Back home in Ohio, these Quakers had decided to sail their boat from California to Hawaii and then out into the testing area where they themselves could be exposed to the radiation. They hoped that this would call people's attention to the testing and rally people to help stop it. They had reached Hawaii and were getting their boat ready for the final lap of their journey when the authorities told them they could not continue. When it was clear they were going to disobey the order and go anyway, they were arrested.

Barbara and Earle were impressed by their courage. Having seen for themselves the terrible and lasting damage one US nuclear bomb had caused to the city of Hiroshima and its people, they too believed that nuclear weapons should never be used again. They wanted to call people's attention to the danger of the US nuclear program. Should they finish the trip that the *Golden Rule* had tried to take?

They held a family council and decided that they should sail the *Phoenix* into the testing zone. Their daughter Jessica was 14; their son Ted was 19. Both children insisted on participating in the protest instead of staying on shore with friends in Hawaii. They all knew it would be a dangerous trip. They might be exposed to radiation, and they would likely get in trouble with the US military authorities. And it would probably mean the end of Earle's teaching career. But they all agreed it was important to go.

Sailing into the Nuclear Test Zone

They left Honolulu quietly and sailed toward the testing area for nineteen days. On June 30, 1958, a big steel ship, the

US Coast Guard *Planetree* stopped them. They were informed that nuclear bombs were being tested nearby, and there was a regulation against their going into the area.

While all this was being filmed with the family's 8-mm camera, Earle told the Coast Guard commander that they intended to continue into the testing zone. The *Planetree* dropped behind and let them proceed. Two hours later, at 10 PM they entered the zone. They stopped and waited.

The next morning, the *Planetree*'s commander told Earle he was under arrest. Earle asked to sail the *Phoenix* to shore rather than be towed, and this was permitted. The *Phoenix* accompanied the *Planetree* to the island of Kwajelein.

The seas were rough, the weather rainy. While Barbara and Ted took their watch, a huge, dark orange flash appeared in the distance. It was one of the nuclear bombs going off.

The next day, they arrived at Kwajalein, and a few days later, Earle, Barbara, and Jessica were flown under guard to Honolulu. They left the *Phoenix* in the care of Ted and Nick Mikami, a Japanese crewman who had helped them on their world trip.

Earle, as skipper of the *Phoenix*, was charged with violating the International Atomic Energy Commission's regulation against going into the testing zone. That was a felony, with a penalty of up to two years in jail and a $5,000 fine. Although he was released on bail awaiting his trial, Earl was not permitted to go to Kwajelein to sail the *Phoenix* back to Hawaii.

After all her recent sailing experience, Barbara courageously set off to retrieve the *Phoenix* with Ted and Nick. The winds were so strong and unpredictable that it took them 60 days and a nearly 4,000-mile route to sail back to Honolulu. Barbara had never been at sea so long. When Earle hugged her at the end of the long trip, she sobbed with relief.

During this time, Barbara's whole way of thinking about herself and her world was changing. No longer could she think of herself as just a mother and a writer of mysteries and children's books. She had become an activist, concerned about the fate of her country and the whole world, with a new feeling of personal responsibility for spending her own life energy to do whatever she could to end the risk of a nuclear war. She was convinced that a nation with nuclear weapons might sometime be tempted to use them.

Public opinion about their action in sailing into the test zone ranged from praise and thanks for trying to eliminate nuclear bombs and their testing to criticism for breaking the law and endangering their children. Supporters of their cause sent them money to help them with their efforts and their legal expenses. It was during this time that Barbara became a Quaker.

Hiroshima Again

Earle was convicted but appealed and won, challenging the legitimacy of the regulation. In 1960 the family sailed back to Hiroshima, where they continued to live on their boat. While Earle worked to establish a Peace Research Institute, Barbara visited survivors who were still in the A-Bomb Hospital and in other places in the area. She listened to their stories as best she could. Despite her poor Japanese, her prayerful presence and friendly smile communicated her interest in them and in what they were still suffering from their ordeal fifteen years before.

One woman told of going into the city with a cart three days after the bombing to try to find the daughter of a neighbor. She found the girl in a first-aid station near the mission school. The woman said,

> When I went in and called her name, Sachiko, she answered faintly. Her face had been burned badly and was covered with a handkerchief, but she said she was Sachiko. As I pushed her back home on the cart, it was dark and you could see fires all over the city and on the mountains. The fires were burning

dead bodies. I took the girl home, but she died. The handkerchief was stuck to the girl's face, and her mother could not remove it. The girl died without her mother ever seeing the face, and the mother refused to believe it was her daughter. Until that time, I had felt nothing, just that I had to take care of my neighbor, but when I brought the girl back and the mother would not accept her, some human feeling began to return. But I still only moved through the day.

Another woman described how some people had just disappeared from the extreme heat of the nuclear blast. Even today, in Hiroshima, there are visible shadows, etched into the concrete walls, where people were when the blast occurred.

Traveling with Hibakusha

Survivors of the nuclear bombing are called *hibakusha* (pronounced hibaak shaa). Barbara thought that if people in western countries could meet *hibakusha* in person and hear their stories, public opinion against the use of nuclear weapons would increase. In 1962 she arranged to take two young *hibakusha* to the United States, Europe, and the Soviet Union, and two years later, she took fifteen interpreters and twenty-five more *hibakusha*, both men and women. This time they were from both Hiroshima and Nagasaki, which had suffered nuclear bombing a few days after Hiroshima. They asked for world peace in eighteen countries, including the United States and the Soviet Union. The trip lasted three months, and Barbara paid for it herself with money she had inherited.

It was a disappointing experience. A few people actually accused her of aiding the enemy in bringing these Japanese women to speak. In each country people offered excuses for not responding positively to the messages brought to them by these women who had lost so much from the nuclear bombing of their city.

In Europe, they were told,

Hundreds of our cities were completely destroyed too. In Dresden alone, more people were incinerated in the massive incendiary raids than were killed in Hiroshima. And what about the extermination camps—Auschwitz and Dachau and Sachsenhausen and the rest? (Japan was an ally of Nazi Germany in the war.)

In Russia:

Don't forget Leningrad and Stalingrad! Russia lost 20 million people during World War II. We saw whole villages of old people, women, and children ruthlessly exterminated before our eyes. You don't have to talk about the suffering of war— and we know, too, what country was responsible for the dropping of the atomic bomb.

In China:

No more Hiroshima! We must destroy the enemies of peace— even if we have to use nuclear weapons to do it!

In Indonesia, Singapore, and the Philippines:

Let them apologize to us! We have memories too of what Japanese did to our homes, to our mothers and sisters, to our country! They only got what was coming to them!

In the United States:

What about Pearl Harbor? Don't forget who started it!

Even in Japan, from their own people:

Stop whining! Are you beggars that you show your scars and recount your troubles, asking for sympathy and cash? Was Hiroshima any worse than hundreds of other Japanese cities that were destroyed by fire raids? They're not still bringing up the past!

Barbara had helped the *hibakusha* find purpose in their own survival when she gave them the chance to go to other countries to share their stories. They were not asking for sympathy for themselves, but for everyone's dedication to future peace for all. Their message had been, "We don't want anyone else to experience what we did! Nuclear weapons are too terrible." They had shown no hatred, no bitterness, no blame, no desire for revenge, though in addition to their own pain and suffering, they had suffered a great deal of discrimination in Japan after the war from people's fear of what genetic damage they might be carrying. But everywhere they went, many people

Barbara with a woman who lost all her family in the bombing of Hiroshima. The woman is holding a doll her grandmother made that the woman had hoped to give her children. She gave it to Barbara, saying "Tell the American women that there is no need to save things to pass on unless we get rid of war."

could think only of their own suffering and their continuing anger and blame for the other side.

The World Friendship Center

In 1965, twenty years after the end of the war, Barbara established a World Friendship Center in Hiroshima in a rented Japanese-style house. In 2004 this center still exists to provide relief activities for *hibakusha* and to share the lessons of Hiroshima. It is a gathering place for *hibakusha*, for Hiroshima citizens, and for visitors from around the world. One of its activities is to visit the A-Bomb Hospital to console patients, whose suffering still continues there after all these years. It also takes visitors to the Peace Memorial Park and Museum, translates materials into English, sends peace missions to other countries, and organizes meetings and peace conferences.

Many years later, Barbara was sure that the voices of the *hibakusha*, raised year after year in reminders and pleas for peace had been important in the fact that nuclear weapons had not been used again up to that time.

In 1969 Barbara left Japan to return to the United States. In 1975, she presented her collection of books, research files, and films in Japanese and English to the newly established Peace Resource Center at Wilmington College, a Quaker College in Wilmington, Ohio. It is the largest collection outside of Japan. On a bookshelf in the office she had there, visitors can see the medal she received in 1975 when she was named an honorary citizen of Hiroshima. At that time she was the first woman and only the fourth person to be given that award.[1]

Barbara receiving her Citizen of Hiroshima medal from the mayor.

Late in her life, Barbara said, "I am satisfied with my life. I am *hibakusha* myself. My heart is always in Hiroshima till I die."

Going Deeper

Questions to Ponder

1. How does Barbara's life speak to you?
2. At first, Barbara resisted the idea of sailing around the world because of her fear of the sea. Have you had an

---

[1] Another was Quaker Floyd Schmoe, whose story begins on page 108.

experience of being pressured to do something big that you didn't think you could do? (ride a bike? sing or recite in front of people?) If you went ahead anyway, what gave you the support you needed? How did you feel afterward?

3. What activist activities have you participated in and what was the experience like?

4. Do you think killing by soldiers is murder? How would you define murder?

Activities

1. Does your community have any remembrance of the atomic bombings on August 6th and 9th? Why is it important to some that these events be remembered every year? What kind of commemoration ceremony would you design?

2. Write a ship's log for the week before and during the *Phoenix's* voyage into the nuclear test zone.

3. Invite an activist to share his/her story with the class or your meeting. The class might organize such an event and introduce the person.

Illustration Credits

Page 74: photograph courtesy of Jessica Shaver.

Page 75: illustration courtesy of Jessica Shaver.

Pages 82 and 83: photographs courtesy of Wilmington College Peace Resource Center.

David Richie and Workcamps
"Work Is Love Made Visible."

by Carol Passmore

I am a member of the Durham Friends Meeting in Durham, North Carolina. When I was a teenager, in the 1950s, I lived in a small town in the South. People didn't travel as much then as they do now, so the only place my family ever went was to visit my grandparents for two weeks every summer. That wasn't enough for me. I wanted to go more places and see new things.

My junior year in high school, when the first black student came to my all-white high school, I became involved in trying to help people learn to be comfortable with black and white children going to the same school and living in the same neighborhoods.[1] That was how I learned about Quakers.

I found that a Quaker organization called The American Friends Service Committee (AFSC) had something they called "workcamps" in New York. I didn't think much about the "work" part or wonder if it was possible to camp in New York City. I just wanted to go.

---

[1] The full story can be found in "New Girl in School" by Carol Passmore in the anthology *Lighting Candles in the Dark: Stories of Courage and Love in Action*, Philadelphia, PA: Quaker Press of FGC, 2001, pp. 152–54.

Workcamping in New York

So the next year I took a train from North Carolina to New York City. I arrived at Grand Central Station. It was grand, all right, the biggest place I had ever seen. My instructions said that I should go to the clock and there I would meet the workcamp leader, Spar Hull, and other teens from around the country. To my surprise, this worked, and soon Spar was leading us down to the subway—the first subway I'd ever been on. When we came back up above ground, we were in Spanish Harlem. This was the first time I'd been around lots of people speaking another language. It was also the first time I'd ever seen houses so close together and big buildings with lots of families living in them and the first time for lots of other things, but that was why I had come to New York City.

It turned out that we actually were camping—sort of— sleeping with several other teens in the Quaker community house and cooking together in the kitchen. And we did work. We worked with families making repairs on their houses or painting their apartments. We also traveled around the city, seeing all the exciting sights and visiting people in organizations like the Quaker Mission to the United Nations. And we talked to people who lived in the neighborhood where we were staying.

One day we were told to go out in pairs and ask anyone who would talk to us some questions about world peace and nonviolence. In the town where I lived, there were only a few people on the street and you probably knew them, but you said hello even if you didn't. In New York City there were thousands of people on the street, all hurrying, and no one said hello. So my partner and I tried to think where people would be sitting, not hurrying, and bored enough to talk to us. We went to a laundromat and found lots of people to answer our questions.

We had a wonderful week, learned lots, and made new friends. But I didn't think about "workcamps," who thought them up, or where else they were happening.

The Beginning of Workcamps

Later I learned that the person who first thought up the idea of workcamps was a Swiss Quaker named Pierre Ceresole. He refused to fight in World War I and tried to get his government to allow peaceful service instead. His government refused, but he organized peaceful service anyway. His first workcamp was near a battlefield in France, where he and pacifist friends from several other countries cleared rubble from the fighting and built houses for people whose homes had been destroyed.

The idea of workcamps came to the United States during the depression in the 1930s. The US government was building a community in Western Pennsylvania for miners who needed better houses. The American Friends Service Committee planned a workcamp to put in a water system for the new community, including a reservoir and several miles of ditches. They wanted to help the miners, but they also were looking for ways to make young people in the United States more aware of the serious social problems in our society. This workcamp had a double purpose—to help with the building project and to give young workcampers a broader understanding of social injustice and inspire them to

David Richie making weavit blankets to send overseas.

want to help our country realize the American dream of fairness and opportunity for all citizens.

Fifty volunteers took part in that workcamp. One of them was David Richie, a young Quaker from New Jersey. Growing up, he had already learned how satisfying it is to help people. His family had taken holiday meals to poor families in Philadelphia, and while he was in college at Haverford, he had worked with children in a poor neighborhood. At the time of this workcamp, he had finished college and was a teacher at Moorestown Friends School.

The workcamp made a deep impression on David. He enjoyed the hard work and felt that what they were doing was important. Another reason he enjoyed it was because he fell in love with one of the other campers, Mary Wright. The last night of the workcamp he asked her to marry him.

They were married the next summer, and eight days later they were leading a workcamp in Philadelphia, helping repair and paint old, broken-down houses. The summer after that, they led a workcamp for high school girls in an Indian boarding school, and the next summer, they went to Mississippi for

David and Mary Richie a few years after they were married.

a workcamp helping sharecroppers—poor families who had no land of their own and worked on other people's land for a share of the crops.

Weekend Workcamps in the City

Then David had an idea. The kids who came to the summer workcamps were kids who could afford to pay for the chance to work without pay, and many of them were already interested in working for social justice. Why not have workcamps just for weekends all through the winter? Many more kids would be able to have the experience of working in poor neighborhoods, including many who had never seen how hard life can be for people in those neighborhoods. The American Friends Service Committee agreed, and for the next thirty years workcamps were held every weekend from October to May. David was at almost all of them. The workcamp I went to in New York was one of David's.

David and workcampers getting supper.

What were these workcamps like, and why were they important? They would start with supper Friday night and end after lunch on Sunday. Each one was planned to do a particular job on a house or apartment, working with the family who lived there. One time the job was to help a family paint their house. The teenage boy in the family was angry, wouldn't do what his mother said, and certainly was not going to help a bunch of strangers paint his house. He stomped out, but David went after him and persuaded him to go along with a few others to get firewood. The boy went unwillingly, but when they returned and he helped unload the wood for his family, he was proud, and he returned to help the next several weekends while the workcampers were working on other houses in his neighborhood. It was a good new experience for him, too.

After enjoying my workcamp in New York so much, I attended four of David Richie's weekend workcamps in an African American church in a small North Carolina town while I was in college. Our job was to dig out a basement under the church so there would be more room for church activities. But the work wasn't the only purpose of the workcamp, or maybe even the main one. The campers were mostly white college students who had never known any black people as friends, and the black members of the church had never known any white people except white bosses. David knew that after four weekends of digging together and four Saturday evenings of wonderful potluck meals and social times afterward, we would be friends and would understand each other much better. He was right.

International Workcamps

Weekend workcamps weren't all that David did, though. In 1946, after World War II, the AFSC asked him to go to Poland to organize an international workcamp. When David's boat sailed into Gdansk, Poland, between the wrecks of many other ships, David was afraid. He was even more afraid when the ship docked and Polish shipworkers swarmed onto the deck and started stealing whatever they could. No one was there to help him guard the AFSC supplies. Even some Polish soldiers who were there did nothing to stop the stealing. When the soldiers started stealing things too, David said the Polish words for "For the children!" He said all the other Polish words he had learned too. The soldiers dropped what they had taken. They went after the shipworkers, who returned the things they had stolen and helped David repack them.

David and his daughter Barbara just after the war. He is about to sail to the Polish workcamp on the Liberty ship you can see in the background.

David's first workcamp in Poland had campers from Switzerland and England as well as Poland. The workcamp was held in a little village called Lucimia that had been totally destroyed in the war. The villagers had been very discouraged but joined eagerly in the work of rebuilding houses in the village and even repaired the school playground. They shared what food they had with the campers.

To teach the campers to be leaders, David had two of them be co-leaders each day. One night the camp was surrounded by angry soldiers who did not understand what was going on.

One of the day's leaders calmly explained what the campers were doing while another camper made a huge pot of cocoa for the soldiers. The soldiers forgot their anger and the next day they brought supplies for the school.

The workcamp movement spread to many countries. David led other workcamps in Poland as well as in Finland and Germany and later in India and Japan and South Africa. He even went to a workcamp in Belgium run by Pierre Ceresole's international workcamp group. David saw much continuing bitterness in these years, so soon after the recent war, but he found that doing helpful hard work together was a wonderful way for people who feared and mistrusted each other to learn to see that of God in each other and even understand each other well enough to be friends.

David and Mary Richie in retirement.

David is 90 years old as this is being written. He is still in touch with many of his former workcampers.

More about Pierre Ceresole

Pierre lived from 1879 to 1945. At 17, he had a mystical experience of which he wrote later,

> I experienced something like a solemn consecration to truth. . . . I was seized by the discovery that to do something constructive in the world one had to be infinitely more sincere, truer, more direct, more alive than the church people, for instance. I was moved to tears. . . . I always remembered that particular day in the woods as a highly important one in my life, as if I had met somebody.

This experience guided him all his life.

All Swiss men were required to serve in the army, but Pierre believed that war is mass murder, inconsistent with Christian principles. There was no provision in Swiss law for conscientious objection, however, and Pierre was repeatedly jailed and fined for refusing to answer the calls to military service. Because he would not fight, many jobs were closed to him, and some people called him a coward.

Pierre was trained in mathematics and philosophy and taught physics for a time. He was restless, though, so he stopped teaching and spent five years traveling around the world, finding other pacifists, working at odd jobs, and giving back most of what he earned to people who needed it.

These were the friends he called to help in that workcamp in France. They had to pay their own way and were given the bare necessities of shelter and food but no pay. Some stayed two weeks, some longer. The project started in November and lasted until spring. They filled holes left by mines and shells, repaired a road, cleared the foundations of the village hall, and built houses and barns. One of the workers was a young man from Germany. He said he had come because the damage had been done by German soldiers, including his own brother. He wanted to help rebuild what they had destroyed.

A few years later there was a terrible flood in Lichtenstein, a tiny country next to Switzerland. Again Pierre sent telegrams to his friends in other countries. He said "Come even if it is impossible." They did. That workcamp lasted six months, and over 700 people from 22 different countries worked with Pierre. Most of them were adults who were pacifists, interested in brotherhood and peace, who had to leave their own jobs to come. In the evenings they would talk about world problems and the need for the peoples of the world to get to know and understand each other and work for peace.

After that, Pierre's Service Civil Internationale had other international workcamps—in France, Switzerland, Spain, and even India, where he got to talk to Gandhi. But he never was able to get his own country of Switzerland to allow peaceful service for conscientious objectors instead of military service.

In his notebooks, he wrote:

God does not punish. He would never get to the end of it. He creates something new.

and

In all earnestness and humility—revise, revise everything, especially your religion. It is a matter of life and death.[2]

Going Deeper

Questions to Ponder

1. How does David's life speak to you?
2. How does Pierre's life speak to you?
3. What should governments do with citizens whose consciences won't let them fight in a war?
4. How was work "love made visible" in these stories?

Activities

1. Design a workcamp project. What would you need to carry it out?
2. If you wanted to participate in a workcamp how would you find out what opportunities exist?

Illustration Credits

Page 87: photograph courtesy of Marty Richie.

[2] Quotations reprinted from "Pierre Ceresole," *Living in the Light, Some Quaker Pioneers of the Twentieth Century*, Volume II, Leonard S. Kenworthy, ed., pp. 19 and 20. Philadelphia, PA: Friends General Conference, 1985. Sources not cited.

Page 88: photograph courtesy of Lois Ledwith Frost, a workcamper.

Page 89: photograph courtesy of Margery Lewis, Philadelphia Yearly Meeting.

Page 91: photograph courtesy of Marty Richie.

Page 92: photograph courtesy of Friends Historical Library, Swarthmore, PA.

Bayard Rustin
Nonviolent Crusader

by Marnie Clark

Bayard Rustin was born in 1912. He was the youngest of twelve children, and grew up in the Quaker home of his grandparents in a small town in southeastern Pennsylvania. His grandfather's father had been a slave. His grandmother was a Delaware Indian who had grown up in Quaker meetings and Quaker schools. It was a close-knit, loving family.

Bayard said his grandmother taught him that "it was too tiresome to hate. We should never go to sleep without reconciling differences that had occurred during the day" and that "nothing constructive was to be gained by arguing over who started what."

His grandmother also taught him that no one is unimportant, that each person should be treated with respect. One day when he was with friends who started making fun of a Chinese family who had a laundry, Bayard joined in the insulting remarks. When his grandmother learned about it, she arranged for Bayard

Bayard at 21, capable and popular despite discrimination.

to spend time after school for the next two weeks helping with the washing and ironing in the laundry.

Achievement, Popularity—and Discrimination

Bayard's town was near the border with Virginia, where slavery had been legal before the Civil War. Although the white communities in his area had welcomed escaping slaves then, all the schools except the senior high school were still segregated, so Bayard went to an all-black school through junior high. It wasn't until he got to senior high school that he began to experience personal discrimination. His best friend, a white boy, was welcome in his home, but Bayard was not allowed to visit in his friend's home. When he went to the movies with his white friends, they could sit anywhere they liked, but he had to sit in one of the two seats in each row that were nearest to the wall. Many of the other black students dropped out of high school because they believed they could never have a good future with everyone looking down on black people.

Not Bayard! He was popular with his classmates and a star player on the basketball, track, and tennis teams. People said he seemed to feel he had to do whatever anyone said he couldn't do—and do it better than anyone else. When someone suggested he go out for football, he did and led the team to an undefeated season for the first time ever! When the team played in a nearby town one day and stopped at a restaurant for lunch, Bayard was not allowed to enter. All his teammates indignantly left the restaurant with him. In another town, the school at first refused to play against a team that had a black player on it, but later they relented and the game was played. When his team practiced at the YMCA in the summer, he could not practice with them because black people were not allowed in the YMCA.

Bayard had an unusually rich tenor voice. He was a soloist in the school chorus. When the chorus won an inter-school contest, however, the judges would not give it the award because they were sure that anyone who sang so well could not be the age Bayard said he was. Though he was valedictorian of his class at graduation and an excellent public speaker and debater, the counselors would not recommend him for a college scholarship.

Bayard, self-confident, finding his path.

Some of the rules that discriminated against black people were just customs that most people had gotten used to and didn't even think about. Some were actually laws, however. Bayard realized that the laws were there because white people generally assumed that black people were inferior and should be kept in their lower place. Bayard knew that he was not inferior. He felt hurt and humiliated and angry when he was treated badly, but he refused to do anything to hurt people who were hurting him. He would not strike back. He was a pacifist but he was not passive. He started looking for ways to call attention to the unfair rules by not cooperating with them.

Challenging Discrimination by Noncooperation

Sometimes he would sit where he wasn't supposed to, or go into a restroom labeled "White" instead of the one labeled "Colored." Sometimes he was physically thrown out. Sometimes he was beaten. Sometimes he was arrested. However badly he was treated, he remained calm and courteous and tried to speak to that of God in the person who was abusing him. He hoped his respectful behavior would appeal to people's consciences so that sooner or later black people would be seen as people of worth and the unfair rules would be changed.

Bayard went to three different colleges but never graduated because he got too interested in working for equality for black people. While he was in one college, he started working for the Young Communist League, which seemed concerned about equal rights for black people. He became disillusioned with them when they changed their entire program after Germany attacked the Soviet Union during World War II. The League suddenly stopped being critical of President Roosevelt and the war and spent all its energy working to defeat Germany to help the Soviet Union. There was no longer any mention of equal rights for black people. Bayard felt that their earlier claims of wanting to help black people were just a way of trying to get more black members for the Communist Party. He was glad he had never become a member of the Communist Party, and he had nothing more to do with Communists after that.

Bayard had considered careers in music, drama, and teaching. Now he decided to put all his effort into being an activist for justice for black people and other minorities. He would use education, organizing, and other nonviolent means. He went to work for the Fellowship of Reconciliation and for other groups formed especially for this work. He took some time out, though, for over a year in prison.

Prison for Draft Refusal

When the military wanted to draft him for the army, he could have been a conscientious objector because of his Quaker background and beliefs. However, he didn't want to cooperate even that much with the military system and was sent to the Ashland Penitentiary in Kentucky. Here, too, he found segregation. Black and white prisoners were not allowed to eat together, and his cell was in the basement of the prison with those of the other black prisoners.

When he protested the separate eating arrangements by joining a hunger strike, he was put in solitary confinement. Eventually, the rule was changed and prisoners were allowed to eat together if they wished.

Bayard had friends in the white section of the prison upstairs and finally received permission to visit them but only on Sundays. One Sunday a white prisoner who didn't like black people mixing with white ones ran at Bayard with a stick and started beating him. Bayard's friends tried to stop him, but Bayard told them not to interfere. The man kept beating Bayard till the stick was shattered. Although it was still usable, the man suddenly stopped, went to a chair, and sat down, shaking all over. He just couldn't go on hitting a man who was not hitting back. He never attacked Bayard again. After that, there were no more restrictions on Bayard's visiting the upper floor on Sunday or any other day.

Bayard was not content only to protest things that were wrong. He got permission to teach classes in reading, writing, dramatics, and music, which the prisoners enjoyed. Most of the white prisoners had never been taught by a black man before. He also made a lute and taught himself to play the guitar while he was in prison.

Bayard taught himself to play the guitar while he was in prison for refusing to be drafted into the army.

Bayard would write later that the other prisoners were brutalized by their prison experience and made to feel guilty whereas the conscientious objector prisoners felt they were making a moral contribution by calling attention to the evil of war. He wrote,

> Still, what is oppressive about prison is that one is unable to be a human being. He is unable to make a single decision about anything he thinks important. A bell rings, and you are permitted to take a shower. A bell rings, and you can go and eat. A bell rings, and you must leave the dining room. A bell rings, and you can go to the library. A bell rings, and you must leave the library. A bell rings and you have no lights at night. A bell rings, and you get up in the morning. A bell rings, and you must leave your cell. A bell rings, and you can go for physical exercise. A bell rings, and you can see the warden. A bell rings, and if you are in the middle of a sentence you must stop talking to the warden. These books you may read, those books you may not read. All of that robs people of their inner capacity to be human beings. And almost all the violence in prison springs from that.[1]

Bayard had been hearing about a man named Gandhi in India who was using what he called "soul force" to persuade the British to let their colony of India be free. Like Bayard, Gandhi would not use violence. He would accept suffering, but he would not make others suffer. And like Bayard, he was looking for ways not to cooperate with unfair rules.

When he got out of prison, Bayard went to India to see what he might learn about Gandhi's methods that would be useful in the struggle for equal rights in this country. Gandhi had been assassinated, but Bayard met and talked to some of Gandhi's friends. He became more convinced than ever that only nonviolent actions would persuade white people in the

---

[1] "Still, what is oppressive": Rustin interview with Columbia University Oral History Project, January 2, 1985, pp. 73–74.

United States to give up their privileges. Although even non-violent actions might frighten them and make them angry, Bayard was sure that violent protests would give them an excuse to crack down with more violence to keep things the way they were.

Direct Challenges to Unfairness

A little later, Bayard and three white friends were arrested for not sitting where they were supposed to on a bus in North Carolina and were put to work on a chain gang. That meant the prisoners were chained together as they worked all day with picks and shovels. It was a terrible experience. They had a pail of water to drink but none for washing. The guards went out of their way to torment the prisoners, sometimes hanging them by their wrists on the bars of their cells with their feet dangling above the ground. A man who misbehaved was punished by being put into a hole in the ground for two or three days with no food or toilet or protection. Once they demanded that Bayard dance for them. When he refused, they used their pistols to shoot at the ground near his feet. Still he refused.

After his release, he wrote a five-part story for *The New York Post* entitled, "Twenty-two Days on a Chain Gang." Not long after that North Carolina changed the law and did away with chain gangs.

Occasionally, his challenges worked right away. Once he went into a restaurant in Indianapolis and asked for a hamburger. The woman said she couldn't serve him. "Why?" he asked. She finally admitted that she was afraid she'd lose business. If people saw him there, they wouldn't come in.

He suggested they try an experiment in extending democracy. He would sit at a table near the door with a hamburger in front of him but would not eat it. For ten minutes they would count the number of people who left or did not come in because of him. If there was one such person, he would leave. If not, he could eat his hamburger.

Bayard waited for fifteen minutes. No one had left, and a couple had come in, paying no attention to him. The woman brought him a hot hamburger. "What would you like to drink?" she asked.

Helping Martin Luther King, Jr.

One Friday afternoon in 1955 in Montgomery, Alabama, a young black woman named Rosa Parks got on a bus and sat down in the front seat where black people were not allowed to sit. The bus got more crowded and pretty soon there were white people standing. The driver ordered her to get up and give her seat to a white person. When she politely refused, he had her arrested.

Over the weekend the black people of the city heard about it and decided not to use the buses to get to work. This would be a hardship for them because most had no cars and many lived several miles from their jobs. But a group of black people calling themselves the Montgomery Improvement Association set about organizing rides, and an inspiring young preacher, Martin Luther King, Jr., was chosen to lead the boycott. Within a month he was arrested and convicted for driving 35 miles an hour in a 25-mile-an-hour zone. His house was bombed. But the protest continued.

Bayard went to Montgomery to help. After his house was bombed, Dr. King had gotten a gun. Bayard helped him to see that any violence on his part or that of his protectors, even if it was provoked by the police, would be fatal for the movement, whereas if this peaceful bus boycott were successful, it could be the beginning of a nation-wide movement toward equality.

One night Dr. King was so discouraged that he talked about giving up. "I can't go on," he said. "These people can't walk any more. Where are we going to get more cars?" Bayard went to nearby Birmingham and got some of the steelworkers there to lend cars for carpooling. He also raised money from sympathetic organizations in the north. The protest went on.

For over a year the black people of Montgomery refused to ride the buses. No one had dreamed it would go on so long. Finally, seeing how much money the buses and the downtown stores were losing, the city gave in and changed the law. Black people could sit wherever they liked on buses and could no longer be made to give up their seats to white riders. They had proved that a bad system could be changed by noncooperation and that change could start when one person refused to cooperate with an unfair rule.

Bayard continued to advise Dr. King, help him with his writing and public appearances, and organizing more support for the movement. He also helped the American Friends Service Committee arrange for Dr. and Mrs. King to go to India to learn more about Gandhi's ideas and nonviolent actions.

In the South in this country, however, Bayard had to stay in the background, often out of sight, because the FBI had discovered his earlier work with the Young Communist League. They wanted to discredit Dr. King by calling him a communist and trying to make people believe that communists were causing all this "trouble" in the South over black people's "rights." Also, Bayard was gay, and many people thought homosexuality was immoral. Bayard didn't want his reputation to interfere with the people's support for Dr. King.

But Dr. King valued Bayard's help and ideas and his ability to organize protests. Bayard was also training many people to remain nonviolent even when they were attacked. People all over the country were becoming more aware of the protests. They were seeing on television the courage of black people

marching peacefully and being attacked by angry white people and police using dogs, cattle prods, and fire hoses.
Meanwhile, federal authorities were realizing that new civil
rights laws were needed, and northern businesses were beginning to put pressure on their southern companies to treat
their black and white workers equally.

Planning the 1963 March on Washington

By 1963 the country was ready for a national march on
Washington "for jobs and freedom." Bayard was given the task
of organizing it. It was a huge job and he had less than two
months to do it. He had to mobilize 100,000 people around
the country, from political, labor, and religious groups; plan for
planes, trains, and 1,500 buses; have thousands of simple bag
lunches prepared by volunteers; have ambulances, first-aid sta-
tions, mobile toilets, microphones, and loudspeakers in place;

A peaceful, joyous crowd surrounded the area where Martin Luther King, Jr.
gave his famous "I have a dream" speech, August 28, 1963, Washington, DC.

and reconcile the different ideas of the ten different groups who were to have speakers. After he consulted with the White House, it was arranged that there would be national guard, army, and marine personnel nearby, but that there would be no uniformed police with guns within the 180-acre area of the demonstration.

So many entertainment celebrities volunteered to come that Bayard made them part of the program. He had to plan the sequence of events and get instructions to participants and publicity to the press. The march would all take place on one day. People must arrive after 6 AM and leave by 6 PM. There would be no sit-ins or civil disobedience. Only signs provided by the organizing committee could be carried. Only with such very detailed planning could confusion and chaos be avoided; even so, many people feared there would be violence.

On the appointed day a quarter of a million people came. It was a happy, hopeful crowd, and there was no violence. They overflowed the whole area around the tidal basins between the Washington Monument, where the entertaining celebrities performed first, and the Lincoln Memorial, where the leaders then spoke in turn. The last speaker was Martin Luther King, Jr. who ended with the famous speech, "I have a dream."

The next year Dr. King's leadership and moral authority were recognized internationally when he was awarded the Nobel Prize for Peace. Bayard traveled to Oslo with him for the acceptance ceremony.

After that, Bayard's efforts were often focused on helping struggling groups in other countries—the Solidarity Movement in Poland, the work against apartheid in South Africa, and efforts to establish democratic systems in Ghana, Tanzania, and other African countries. There, too, he helped people demonstrate the power of nonviolence to right wrongs and change unfair systems. He died in 1987.

Going Deeper

Questions to Ponder

1. How does Bayard's life speak to you?
2. What do you think made Bayard able to respond to insults with respect instead of bitterness?
3. Have you ever been excluded from a group or activity because of something that was not your fault? How did it feel? Have you ever excluded others because they were different?
4. Do you think you could accept being beaten and not hit back? Does it take more courage to hit back or not to hit back?

Activities

1. Find out more about Bayard Rustin using the library or the internet.
2. Pick an issue and plan a demonstration in your community. What would you need to carry it out?
3. How many other famous African American Quakers can you name?

Illustration Credits

Page 96: photograph courtesy of Friends Historical Library, Swarthmore, PA.

Page 98: photograph courtesy of Swarthmore College Peace Collection, Swarthmore, PA.

Page 100: photograph courtesy of Swarthmore College Peace Collection, Swarthmore, PA.

Page 105: photograph by Nat Herz, © Barbara Singer, www.barbarasinger.com, New York, NY.

Floyd Schmoe
105 Years of Zest and Service

by Marnie Clark

"Always have something exciting to do tomorrow," Floyd Schmoe said when in his nineties. Floyd never expected to be milking goats on a ship in the middle of the Pacific Ocean. He was on a Heifer Project ship taking the goats to Japanese farmers. It was just after World War II. The United States had dropped a nuclear bomb on Hiroshima, which destroyed the city and killed thousands of people. Floyd was so horrified that he felt he had to go to Hiroshima to help people there who were still alive. Over the next four years Floyd and his friends built 40 houses for Hiroshima families. He was fifty years old when he started. He said he was just doing what his "inner radar" told him to do. That was Floyd's lifetime pattern.

Rural Kansas in the Early 1900s

He knew how to milk goats because he had grown up on a farm in a small Quaker community in Kansas. Six generations of his family had been Quakers. Floyd was born in 1895, only a few years after Kansas had become a state. Where he lived, everyone helped everyone and children helped with the farm chores. They had no electricity, no television or computers, no frozen food or pizza. There was only one store in town, with a post office in the back.

Floyd loved the out-
doors and was curious
about everything. He
roamed the area, collecting
birds' eggs, leaves, flowers,
the occasional arrowheads
he found, and even fossils
from the time long ago
when that land had been
under an ocean. On a
trip to California he
learned that woodpeckers
in California would drill
hundreds of holes in tree

Floyd and his wife Ruth when they were
about 50 (1944).

trunks and stuff acorns into them for winter food, whereas
Kansas woodpeckers didn't do that. Evidently, they got
enough food from fruit, insects, and grubs in rotten branches.
He became fascinated with the ways creatures adapt to what
different environments provide and demand.

When he was eight years old, there were heavy rains and
the river near them overflowed its banks. Floyd's house was
safe, but when his family hitched their old horse Charlie to
the buggy and drove to the bluff to look, they saw swirling
brown water for miles. Drowned horses and cows, farm
implements, and even parts of houses were being carried
down the rushing river. A little later they heard the news of
the terrible earthquake in San Francisco.

From these experiences Floyd learned how fragile life is.
He realized that we cannot just take it for granted. He
decided he wanted to do whatever he could to make life safer
and better for people. Floyd's mother helped him think of the
Inner Light as a guide that would help him see the right thing
to do. Radar hadn't been invented yet then, but later Floyd
liked to think of his Inner Light as a kind of radar.

Floyd knew he wanted an outdoor career. After high school he went to Seattle to study forestry at the university. When they told him that he had to enroll first in the Reserve Officers' Training Corps (ROTC), he was furious. As a Quaker, he didn't want to have to take military training. Luckily, a sympathetic dean organized an Ambulance Corps, so Floyd was able to learn how to rescue injured soldiers instead.

Ambulance Corps Worker in France

The ambulance training came in handy when the United States entered World War I. Floyd was sent to France to work with the American Friends Service Committee (AFSC) and British Friends. His job was to unload injured soldiers from trains and take them to the hospital. It was hard work and dangerous, too. Once the blast from an exploding shell tossed him out of a truck. Another time, he came up out of a subway shelter only to be knocked back down the stairs by the force of a shell exploding not far away. Sometimes there were so many injured soldiers that he had to work 30 hours without sleep. One night a bomb blew up a block away, but he was so exhausted he didn't even wake up.

Besides transporting wounded soldiers, Floyd helped build houses for refugees. He was unhappy that there was no safe place for children to play, so he built a playground for them. When it was opened, so many children came that they had to take turns going into it to play—20 children at a time,

When the war ended, there was a call for volunteers to take a trainload of medical supplies and food to Poland. Floyd and three other young men volunteered. They were on the train over a month, because the engines had to keep being changed. When they crossed into Germany, they were stopped and held at bayonet point while soldiers broke into every one of their cartons to see if any contained weapons or munitions.

Of course none did. Finally the train was allowed to proceed. At one place the people didn't know the war was over and were still fighting against each other, so the train spent a few days being fired over. When they finally got to Warsaw, they were treated like heroes. The premier of Poland even gave them seats in his box at the opera.

Park Naturalist and Student of Underwater Ecololgy

As soon as he got back to the United States, Floyd married Ruth Ann Pickering, his high school sweetheart, and they both enrolled in classes in Seattle at the University of Washington—she in music and he in forestry. When he got his forestry degree, he became Mount Rainier's first park naturalist and worked there for ten years. Then he got a chance to give programs in Pugent Sound and the San Juan Islands for people who wanted to learn more about science and nature—a lot of what we call ecology today. He built a hollow cement ball with windows on the sides that he could lower into the water. From it, he took the first color pictures of life under the water.

Later he built a houseboat in which the biggest window was the floor of the living room. His family and his students liked to watch the marvelous community of marine plants and animals beneath them as the boat moved along. By that time he and Ruth Ann had four children.

AFSC Service Again

In the late 1930s war clouds were gathering in Europe. Floyd was teaching at the University of Washington by then. Much as he enjoyed his job, he resigned it to volunteer for the AFSC again, this time helping people who were being hurt by Hitler and the Nazis. Jews were in special danger, and the AFSC was helping many to escape from Germany before it was too late.

Then the Japanese bombed Pearl Harbor and the United States entered the war. In their shock and anger, many people were afraid that the Japanese army would invade California and that the Japanese-Americans who lived near the coast would help them. So all people of Japanese ancestry who lived near the West Coast were told they would be deported to "detention" camps even though most of them were US citizens. They would have to leave their homes and businesses behind, as well as everything else they could not cram into a few suitcases.

The AFSC put Floyd to work finding places in eastern schools and universities where Japanese-American teachers and students could go and thus not be sent to the camps. He also found farms that would take Japanese-American farmers. Over 4000 people were helped in this way. Floyd and others at AFSC also did what they could to protect homes and property that Japanese-American families had to leave behind. After the war, when they were released and allowed to go back home, the AFSC volunteers welcomed them, painted over hate signs that had been put up, and helped them replant their fields. Volunteers who sympathized with the Japanese-Americans and helped them were sometimes in danger because some people hated everything Japanese and blamed them for the war.

Building Houses in Hiroshima

When the war was over, Floyd found a way to get to Japan by milking goats on a Heifer Project ship. When he got to Hiroshima, the mayor told him he could build a library for books that the US soldiers were donating. Floyd thanked him, but didn't think that books in English were what the Japanese children needed most. He told the mayor that what he wanted to do was build houses for people who had survived the atomic bombing but had lost their homes.

Floyd being interviewed by a class of 6th-graders in Hiroshima, Japan during house building.

Eventually, Floyd was able to arrange to build houses with friends from Seattle and many Japanese volunteers. Instead of building the kinds of houses they would have built in the United States, they wanted to build houses in which Japanese families would feel comfortable. A Japanese architect worked with them to design Japanese-style houses. They put some parts of the houses together at the lumber store and then carried the big sections through the town to where all the parts of each house would be put together. A stone mason helped them with foundations and steps. They learned how to split bamboo and fit the pieces into the upright parts. Then they put stucco and whitewash on the outside. They also planted vegetable gardens.

Honorary Citizen of Hiroshima

There was an interesting sequel to this adventure. Years later, Floyd was invited back to be made an honorary citizen of Hiroshima and to receive a medal from the emperor of Japan. During the ceremony, a note was handed to him. It was from the chief of police, asking him to come to the police station after the ceremony. Floyd wondered what terrible thing he had done. Was he going to be arrested?

When he got to the police station, the chief said, "Thirty-five years ago you built a house for my family. We are still living in it. This is my first chance to say 'Thank you.'"

During his long life Floyd helped make life better for people in several other countries. For example, after the Korean War, the United Nations sent Floyd to build houses and a clinic in Korea. The first doctor in the clinic was a volunteer from Floyd's Quaker meeting in Seattle. Floyd also helped build hospitals and orphanages in Kenya and Tanzania. After the first Arab-Israeli war he went to Egypt to restore damaged wells in the desert so that people could have water again. With money that was left over, he bought and planted fruit trees.

Sadako and the Seattle Peace Park

When he was 91, Floyd visited Hiroshima again and saw the statue of Sadako, with thousands of paper cranes piled on it. Sadako was a 12-year-old girl who was badly burned by the nuclear bomb the United States dropped on Hiroshima. She believed that if she could fold 1,000 paper cranes, she would get well, but she died before she could finish that many. Her friends completed the thousand cranes and tucked them in around her when she was buried. A beautiful statue of her was put in the Hiroshima Peace Park. Her arms are stretched up over her head with her fingers touching the wings of a dove and the words, "I will write peace on your wings and you shall fly to all the world." Every year thousands of children from all over the world bring and send paper cranes to be placed on and around her statue.

After his trip Floyd decided that Seattle should have a Peace Park. When he got home, he found a tiny spot near the canal where hundreds of students would pass by every day. No one had paid any attention to it and it was covered with weeds and trash, but Floyd was not discouraged. He got permission to make a little park there and set to work clearing out the cans, bottles, and weeds. He also studied historical records to find what kinds of bushes and trees were native to that area. As he worked, he kept thinking how wonderful it would be to have a statue of Sadako. He couldn't imagine how that would be possible.

Floyd at the dedication of the Seattle (WA) Peace Park (left) and his statue of Sadako, draped with paper cranes (right).

Two years later he was invited to Hiroshima again to receive a special peace prize. While he was there, he had tea with the crown prince and princess of Japan and was told that his prize included $5,000! You will not be surprised to learn that when he got home, he used his prize money to have a statue of Sadako made for his peace park. This one would not be up on a pedestal like the one in Hiroshima, however. He wanted it down on the ground where people could touch it.

Floyd was 95 years old when the Seattle Peace Park was dedicated. He was happy to see that children were bringing paper cranes to put around Sadako's statue. He lived ten more years, and he continued to work in his little park every day as long as he could. He said,

> Hoping for and believing in peace is easy when my hands are in the good earth. Our business is to be the co-creators, the hands and feet, the instruments of God.

Floyd's Grandmother's Breakfast Cereal

Floyd's grandmother figured out a way of making breakfast cereal out of oats. It was sold as "Purity Oats." Later it was bought by a company that still calls it "Quaker Oats."

Going Deeper

Questions to Ponder

1. How does Floyd's life speak to you?
2. Describe an experience of having "inner radar." What did it feel like? What did you do?
3. What are some themes in Floyd's long and full life?

4. What kind of peace memorials have you seen or vis-
    ited? How about war memorials?

Activities

1. What would it take to create a peace memorial in your
    community? See www.sadako.org/seattlepeacepark.htm
    to learn more about how Floyd built his park.
2. Research and consider organizing a fundraising effort
    for the Heifer Project.
3. Read the story *Sadako and the Cranes* then retell the
    story in your own words.

Illustration Credits

All illustrations for this chapter courtesy of Judy Rudolf.

Carol Reilley Urner
Find a Need and Act on It

by Barbara Robinson

During her 74 years, living in seven countries, often unable to speak the local language, Carol has always found a way to tackle a serious social problem to make life better for people who were suffering.

Carol Reilley was born in 1929. She says that from being taught to pray by her mother and listening eagerly to Bible stories her father read to her, the Inward Teacher became real to her when she was only two or three. She remembers a strong spiritual insight that came to her when she was about five. She was struck with the meaning of God's command, "Thou shalt not kill." Death is no game. We must not kill.

A Leading for a Lifetime

This insight carried Carol into her teen years and World War II. When the United States got into the war, the government started to sell war stamps. If you were patriotic, you bought war stamps to support the government. Carol wrote poems and articles for her school paper, urging other students to buy

Carol Reilley Urner.

war stamps. Many students donated their lunch money to buy the stamps. Carol did so too at first. Then she realized that buying war stamps was giving money for bombs and bullets.

This created a dilemma for her. In Matthew 5, verses 44–45, Jesus says, "Love your enemies." How could she support her country's war and obey God at the same time? Carol suddenly understood that there would be times when she would have to go

Carol at seventeen.

against ideas and actions that her friends and even her country supported in order to act on the light God was giving her. She stopped buying war stamps and encouraging others to do so. This was a hard thing for her to do. It is hard to resist pressure from your friends, hard to say "No" when most people around you are demanding a "Yes."

Carol was growing up during a time when some people were struggling with the idea that God was dead. They were saying that religion was meaningless and out of date. It was a difficult time, especially for young people who were trying to find a faith to live by.

In college, Carol's desire to help people in need led her to work with children who had cerebral palsy. She also went to American Friends Service Committee weekend workcamps. There she met Quakers and began attending meeting for worship. She learned about the testimonies and read what Friends like George Fox, William Penn, and Isaac Pennington had written. She was especially drawn to the writings of John Woolman.

Quakers' belief that God's light dwells in each of us, was what first led her to Quakerism. She stayed with Friends because she found them a listening people who acted on what they heard. The Quakers she saw seemed to be trying sincerely to live the gospel way.

Carol and Jack

Carol focused on listening more closely to her Inward Guide. Her sense of God's presence became stronger. She says that one evening, as she was saying good-night to a young man named Jack, she heard a distinct, audible voice saying, "Marry this man." She saw a soft light shining on Jack's face. Could God be talking to her? A few weeks later, they became engaged, and in 1952 they married.

Carol and Jack were in their twenties then. They were sad that the world did not seem to hear the message Jesus taught, the message they were hearing so strongly, about the preciousness of every person and the need for peace. They saw the Quakers around them as living examples of the kind of lives they wanted to lead. They joined the Religious Society of Friends together.

Jack knew he could not kill another human being so he sought conscientious objector status. Carol helped him go through graduate school to learn how to help people in poor countries have better lives. Their son Kirby was born in 1958; their daughter Julie followed three years later.

In the years after the war, the United States became wealthy and powerful. There were many new inventions. Television arrived, with commercials urging people to buy, Buy, BUY! These were also the years of an intensifying "cold war." The United States and the Soviet Union raced in developing more nuclear weapons. It was a scary time. Meanwhile, the wealthy countries were often taking advantage of people in the poor countries. In fact, more money was flowing from the poor countries to the rich ones than the other way around because it was the rich ones and their businesses that had enough money to get at natural resources like oil and minerals and control trade.

In the early 1960s Carol feared that because of the increase in nuclear weapons her children might never have a chance to grow up. She wrote a letter to the local paper about her concerns and many other women responded and joined her in a women's peace movement. She began to do many things she had never done before, like giving speeches on radio and television, marching in street demonstrations, visiting senators and the mayor and governor. She even traveled to Hiroshima and the Hague to speak against preparations for war.

Jack supported her efforts, and although she often felt stretched and challenged, she also felt she was held in God's hand. Looking back years later, Carol and Jack felt the movement had really helped waken people in the United States to the need to stop nuclear testing and prevent nuclear war.

Libya and Beyond

In 1964 Jack was sent to Libya to help plan the country's development. During the six years he worked there, Carol and the children lived in Rome, across the Mediterranean Sea from Libya, where Jack often was. The children went to school and Carol studied history and wrote a novel about St. Francis. She also worked with the Sisters of Mother Teresa, caring for poor people. She felt God was helping her learn and grow more deeply in the Spirit—preparing her for her future service.

In 1972 they had a brief time in Israel, working for the American Friends Service Committee. Their work was trying to help Israelis and Palestinians build bridges of understanding after so many years of fighting. Living in a Jewish kibbutz they learned the pride Israelis felt in their new country. Living in tents with Palestinians, they learned how difficult it is to live in a country controlled by someone else.

The next year they moved half way around the world to the Philippines. Here, as in many places, they found wealthy people taking advantage of native people, cheating them out of valuable land. Carol wasted no time. She joined with Catholic sisters and Protestant lay people to help the indigenous people win back their land and their rights. In their work they taught nonviolent ways of settling disputes. They insisted on truthfulness and openness in all discussions, taking the same message to everyone—the military, the rebels, and civilians. Carol was practicing what she had learned from the Sisters of Mother Teresa—to go to the poorest people and to be willing to live at the bottom with them. From Jesus and Gandhi, however, she had also learned to speak the truth to people in power.

Six years later Jack's work took them to Egypt. Here again, Carol looked for a need and how she mght act on it. She began to work with people at the bottom of the society— people living in a garbage dump who were known as "the Zabbaleen." They were Coptic Christians who raised pigs and ate pork. Most Egyptians are Muslims, and Muslims do not eat pork. They had long despised the Zabbaleen as "pig raisers." The Zabbaleen had been chased off their land and were living in an abandoned quarry where they collected garbage to feed their pigs and survive.

Carol got some money from the Quaker Right Sharing of World Resources project and helped the Zabbaleen organize a cooperative to make money from collecting garbage. Cairo is a large city and there is a lot of garbage. Soon the World Bank made larger loans that enabled the Zabbaleen to set up a garbage collection company for the whole city. Carol found volunteers to help. The Sisters of Mother Teresa helped too, and that was when Carol got to meet Mother Teresa herself—

a memory she will always cherish. The Zabbaleen recycle much of the garbage now. They are no longer so poor and the Egyptian government allows them to own land, where they are building houses, clinics, and schools.

From 1983 to 1985 Jack and Carol lived in Bangladesh, another Asian country, where many people were starving and there were frequent floods and typhoons. Carol asked God for a project working with very poor people. Soon she found a Dutch woman who had begun a medical clinic for desperately poor women, children, beggars, and prostitutes.

Carol helped in the clinic, but she realized that the women also needed income to keep themselves and their children alive. She helped start a sewing cooperative where mothers and their children also learned to read, write, and count. Quaker Right Sharing of World Resources sent money to help buy sewing machines and a loom. Many volunteers helped and Carol remembers the loving sisterhood that developed between wealthy women and poor women working together.

Bhutan and Lesotho

Next, Carol and Jack moved to Bhutan, a very small country in the Himalayan mountains in Asia. Bhutan has a king who has all the power and does not allow volunteer organizations to work in his country. That didn't stop Carol. She asked the king for permission to teach and was given a job teaching a third-grade class of 76 children for $40 a month. She taught there for five years. She was dissatisfied with the materials the school provided, so she wrote a new curriculum. It was so successful that she wrote a curriculum for the whole country. She trained teachers too, which amused her because she had never had teacher training herself. By then the Bhutanese thought she could do it, she loved doing it, and it seemed to work well.

Carol remembers her time in Bhutan as truly wonderful. She saw how her Christian beliefs paralleled Buddhist teachings to live compassionate lives and lessen the suffering of all creatures. But alas, beliefs do not always translate into the behavior you would expect. The king was afraid that the Hindus and Christians would destroy Bhutan's Buddhist faith, so there came a time of "ethnic cleansing" when many people were killed or driven out.

In 1993 Carol and Jack went to live in Lesotho, a little country in southern Africa with many mountains. For two years, Jack helped the country develop primary schools, but then he retired. They didn't want to leave and felt they could still be useful, so they decided to stay. This time they changed positions, with Carol working in a job in the US embassy and Jack doing volunteer work in the community. After many years under a military dictatorship,

Carol and Jack in LeSotho.

Lesotho became a democracy soon after apartheid ended in nearby South Africa in the mid-1990s. Carol helped many organizations with small human rights grants to help build fairness and equal rights in Lesotho.

In 1998 Carol retired too, and they talked about leaving at last, but then there was an attempted coup. Many non-Buddhist citizens were driven out and became refugees with no country of their own. Carol and Jack decided they must stay to help, and Carol became a full-time Quaker volunteer with a Lesotho Christian human rights agency. It was satisfying but dangerous work. There are not many good roads in Lesotho. Jack drove Carol over narrow, rocky mountain trails to deliver materials on education for democracy to students in two hundred high schools.

It was in South Africa, however, on a very good road, that a small truck suddenly crossed into their lane for a head-on collision. Jack was killed and Carol was injured so badly that she was not expected to live. She felt held in God's hand, however, and surprised the doctors. Her children brought her back to the United States to recuperate. She misses her husband of 48 years but believes God arranged their lives well. She says, "God holds us, teaches us, needs us, and uses us with all our failings and imperfections for the work that needs doing."

Carol Today

Carol still uses a walker but has otherwise recovered from her injuries. When she regained consciousness after the accident, she knew that she was meant to come back to the United States to work on demilitarization. She now chairs the National Disarmament Campaign of the Women's International League for Peace and Freedom (WILPF). This organization has won two Nobel Peace Prizes and has always included many Quaker women.[1] Carol flies around the country taking part in conferences with representatives of other non-governmental organizations that are working for disarmament and peace. She does research, writes materials, uses a website, meets with congress people, gives speeches, and helps organize anti-war demonstrations. She is horrified at the new weapons of death being created with our tax dollars. She believes God needs all of us, old and young, to help create peace in the world. She says

[1] Stories about two other Quaker women who have been active in WILPF are on pages 10 (Elise Boulding) and 157 (Emily Greene Balch).

Jesus showed us the way, and that the Comforter is always there to guide us, even when the tasks seem very difficult.

She carries her reputation as an authority with humor and lightness. She has not stopped writing either, and is widely known for articles she has written for *Evangelical Friend*, *Friends Journal*, and *Quaker Life*, as well as pamphlets for Pendle Hill.

Moving from country to country and culture to culture, Carol often lived without many of the things we take for granted. She experienced new languages, new governments, and new religions. In each place she prayed to God for new tasks to work on—new paths to usefulness. Today she says,

> It was a privilege to meet and know so many different people in so many different countries. Though most were poor, they were amazingly generous. They knew and expressed the values of love and care.

Those are the values Carol knows and expresses. It is of these that her life speaks.

Going Deeper

Questions to Ponder

1. How does Carol's life speak to you?
2. What is one thing that many of your friends do that you've decided not to do because you think it's wrong? In what ways is it hard for you to be different?
3. How would you feel if your family was going to move to another country for two years? How would you try to make it a worthwhile time in your life?
4. "Give a man a fish and he will eat for a day. Teach him to fish and he will eat for a lifetime." How does this proverb relate to Carol's work?

Activities

1. Carol has written several articles in Quaker journals. Four were in *Friends Journal* June 1983, March 1990, and July 1995; and in *Quaker Life* December 1997. Read and discuss one of these articles.
2. Pick one thing from this story that intrigued you. Do some research about it. Did what you found out make you more or less interested?
3. On a map of the world locate the countries where Carol and Jack lived and worked.

Illustration Credits

Page 118: photograph courtesy of *Friends Journal*.
Pages 119 and 124: photographs courtesy of Carol Reilley Urner.

Gilbert White
Using Science to Help People

by Gilbert White; adapted by Jeanette Baker

Gilbert White, at age 91, tells about a conversation he remembers that took place when he was ten years old:

I was helping weed a vegetable garden with my Uncle Gilbert. We had been talking about my recent activities at school—sports teams, friends, and so on. Suddenly, he asked me a question that surprised me:

"Do you think you will ever amount to anything?"

I wasn't sure what he meant. I knew he wasn't talking about grades or being elected as a class officer or making a lot of money later. Gradually I realized that what he had in mind were things like "Would I have been honest? Would I have helped people? And how would I judge the worth of what I did?" My uncle's question was for me alone. It was a question that I've been considering all my life.

Gilbert White.

From his grandmother Gilbert had heard how his Quaker forebears, coming from Virginia to

Missouri by way of Indiana, had opposed slavery and how they had refused to swear oaths, saying that they would only solemnly affirm. The responsibility was with each person to do what she or he considered right in accord with divine leading. Similarly, only that person could determine whether or not those efforts "amounted to anything."

ROTC and the Question

The question became critical for him when he entered college and had to decide whether or not to sign up for the Reserve Officer Training Corps (ROTC), a military program. He was especially attracted by the opportunity to work with horses. His uncle had been a military officer in World War I and had also worked later in development projects in Siberia, Japan, India, and South Africa. Gilbert knew his parents would not have chosen military service for him, but they said it was up to him. They suggested he could experiment with ROTC and drop out if he didn't feel comfortable.

He did that. Soon after he signed up, the dean of the University Chapel, knowing about his inner searching, invited him to meet a visiting Quaker philosopher, Rufus Jones. From Jones Gilbert heard about how Quakers had organized the American Friends Service Committee to provide ways for young Friends to express their basic beliefs actively in nonmilitary ways. After a great deal of reading and inward searching, Gilbert dropped out of ROTC with a desire to serve people in a way that did not use violence.

The first way he found was to work in a government office in Washington, DC during the depression. It was an exciting time. Roosevelt's "New Deal" was finding ways to help people who had lost everything as well as people who had always been poor and without opportunity. Gilbert and his coworkers felt their work was helping the nation.

Then one day they heard that the Japanese had bombed Pearl Harbor. When he walked into the office the next day, Gilbert found the cabinet staff preparing to declare war. The United States was now joining in World War II, which had been going on in Europe for over two years. Gilbert had to decide whether to stay in the office, where the war effort would be central, or look for some other way to serve his country.

Congress had passed a law prohibiting able-bodied conscientious objectors from leaving the country. Gilbert's draft board had already exempted him from military service because the job he held in the executive office was judged to be "of national importance." So he was allowed to go to Vichy, France, to work with needy people there. Southern France had not yet been conquered by the German army.

Wartime Service

In Vichy, France, he joined a small group of devoted Dutch, French, Irish, Norwegian, and American Quakers who were finding many ways to help people who were suffering because of the war. There were French school children, Jewish children in hostels, and thousands of refugees living behind barbed wire. Jews were already being sent east to the death camps, so the most important service for many Jewish refugees was to try to supply them with visas that would enable them to leave the area.

Other help the Quakers gave included canteens of food, clothes, medical supplies, and an artificial limbs factory to fit amputees with arms or legs so they could get permits to work outside the refugee camps, hostels for stranded children with no family, and help for clusters of refugees in deserted villages. Despite the over-arching sense of tragedy, it felt good to be able to help a little. At the end of the day Gilbert could see children a little less hungry and older folks who now had blankets and medicines. But he also could see tired, helpless people herded up the gangways into cattle cars bound for the death camps in Germany.

In the fall of 1942 the Germans took over the rest of France, closed its borders, and ordered all remaining US citizens to go to Lourdes to stay until the wat was over. Gilbert and another Friend decided not to go right away. Instead, they took control of Quaker supplies that were on the dock in Marseilles and moved them to a small town farther inland where there were good communications. A week later the general staff of the German army moved its office into the same town.

The Germans never bothered Gilbert and his coleague, which puzzled the French citizens in the town. Gilbert learned that the commanding officer, as a boy, had been one of the German children the Quakers had fed after World War I.

The following spring, however, all the remaining US citizens had to go to Baden-Baden, where they spent the next thirteen months. It was like a gilded cage—elegant but without freedom. He had little chance to help anyone except diplomats' children, who did need schooling.

When they finally were sent back to the United States, the AFSC found several ways Gilbert could help people. One way was to raise money for Bengal relief where 2 million people had died the year before in a famine. Another was getting medical help to people trapped in China behind the Japanese lines, where war was still going on. In that assignment, they had to fly supplies and people over the Himalayan mountains from India.

Working to Improve Whole Systems

After the war, Gilbert went to work at Haverford College and later at the University of Chicago and the University of

Colorado at Boulder where the kinds of help he gave were entirely different. In these settings his aim was to plan administration and research in ways that would be really helpful to people. At Haverford, where he was president at age 34, he supported the training of graduate students for relief and rehabilitation work, encouraged undergraduates to participate in the administration of the college, and helped students strengthen the honor system in which they established and enforced their own standards.

Gilbert White, President of Haverford College at the age of 34.

In the universities, Gilbert's focus was on designing and carrying out scientific work that would be useful in improving people's lives. Gilbert believed strongly that it was not enough to aim scientific research just at getting more knowledge. He believed that scientific work must express a constructive concern for ordinary people. The research itself needed to be aimed at making people's lives better.

Gilbert was convinced that for this kind of research to succeed, all the major groups of people who were being affected by a problem would need to work together to solve it, first focusing on understanding all the causes of the problem. For example, in studying why flood damage occurred, the different communities in the area would learn why they would need to work together to prevent destruction of vegetation and safeguard the ecosystem. Because they all would benefit, Gilbert found it was a good way to avoid confrontation and conflict.

This method was used in coordinating and integrating ways of dealing with floodplain problems in the Unites States, where periodic floods, especially along the Mississippi River, have often devastated large areas. It was personally gratifying to Gilbert when a historian of the Army Corps of Engineers said this work reflected a sensitivity to the human condition that was rooted in both Gilbert's training as a geographer and his Quaker faith.

Another example was diagnosing and working to overcome the basic scientific and social problems that the five Asian countries in the Aral Sea Basin shared. The Aral Sea's waters, which they all depended on, were drying up. Study of the whole area led to a plan that became the basis for joint international funding of measures to reduce the water waste, soil destruction, and human suffering in the whole area.

In 1982 a group of scientists launched an effort on a critical international problem under the International Council of Scientific Unions. Its purpose was to explore the environmental effects of a possible nuclear war. The scientists used the same basic approach of having major groups affected by a problem work together. More than 300 scientists from at least 30 countries were involved in discussions over a two-year period. The scientists arrived at a unanimous report that became the basis for a United Nations resolution seeking to outlaw nuclear war. That resolution was adopted unanimously by the UN General Assembly.

Perhaps Gilbert's most continuing and least known efforts to let his life speak his faith have been in Quaker conferences for diplomats. These conferences started in 1952 and brought together diplomats from governments that often have not been in close touch with each other but share some of the same problems. Often they have not understood each other's points of view or had good chances for open communication. The gatherings at diplomat conferences are "off the record." They are never publicized, and no reports are issued. The participants listen to each other and hear one another's point of view. This experience sometimes changes their own thoughts and later their actions. Diplomats continue to come to these meetings at their own expense, which makes Gilbert think that they must find the meetings worthwhile for their own work.

Gilbert chaired the first Quaker Conference for Diplomats with Ralph Bunche, who was well known around the world for his UN work in Palestine and his Nobel Prize for Peace in 1950. Since then there have been many similar gatherings in different parts of the world. Conferences before the important UN Rio Conference on the Environment in 1992 helped to draft the International Convention on Forest Resources.

Studying Access to Water

In the 1960s Gilbert and his wife Anne, in cooperation with a public health expert from the London School of Public Hygiene, undertook the research that he feels was his most important work. The team found that 60 per cent of the world's people still depended on going somewhere every day to get water. Sometimes that meant walking a long way and carrying heavy loads all the way home. Gilbert, Anne, and David Bradley from London studied 34 places in East Africa in a variety of environments to get basic information about what this situation was costing people in time, energy, money, and health.

These problems had never been studied systematically before. As a result of this study, the governments of the region gained a new realization that thousands of people needed better access to safe water. This research was published in a book, *Drawers of Water*, published in 1972. The findings were used by many agencies in developing countries.

Thirty years later, several development agencies financed a repetition of the *Drawers of Water* study to see what progress had been made. Some good things had happened but there

The study repeating Gilbert's original study of how families got their water in East Africa found many families having a shorter walk every day but spending more time having to wait in line at a common tap (bottom left). They all had to carry it a long way home, and even children learned to balance heavy containers on their heads (top left). In cities, many families who had no water piped to their homes had to buy water from traveling vendors (right). More information available at **www.drawersofwater.org**.

were also sobering lessons about what works and what doesn't in helping make water more accessible, especially where it must be obtained outside the home.

Gilbert says,

Looking back at these and other efforts to live my Quaker faith in what I did in my work, I am painfully aware that it didn't always "amount to anything." It might have been easier to judge if I had just concentrated on helping needy people directly. It is more difficult to judge how well I expressed my beliefs and values by applying science to international problems. Perhaps I lacked vision or skill, but I realize that I am the one who finally must use my own standard to judge how much people and their environments have benefitted from what I did.

A few years ago, Gilbert's late wife Anne gave an assessment of her own:

> What makes him keep at this? I think it is all tied together by his Quaker faith in the ability of humans to marshal their inner resources to deal competently and lovingly with the outer world and with their fellow human beings.
>
> Then there is the real fun he gets out of the exchange of ideas with others, and the challenge of making real friends, not just coworkers, out of those others. And not least, there is his innate and humble desire to leave the world a bit better place than he found it.[1]

Recognition of Gilbert's Using Science to Help People

In 2000 the National Academy of Sciences (NAS), awarded Gilbert White its Public Welfare Medal. This award is given each year to honor extaordinary use of science for the public good. Previous recipients of the award include C. Everett Koop and Carl Sagan. The following account appeared in *Quaker Life* that September:

> For seven decades Gilbert White, a member of Boulder Friends Meeting, served as a scientist and a Friend. In April, the National Academy of Sciences presented him with its most prestigious award, the Public Welfare Medal, citing his contributions to environmental studies and public welfare. "By applying science and wisdom to the ways we think about how water is used throughout the world, he has taught us how to recognize the scope of our impact on the environment," said R. Stephen Berry, NAS Home Secretary and Chair of the Selection Committee. Gilbert's scientific work has addressed such areas as flood control and flood-plain management, international water supplies, and ways to reduce human suffering caused by natural disasters. A distinguished

[1] Peter Caughey, "A Quiet Leader," *Summit Magazine*, Winter 1992–93, 17–19. Quote on p.19.

professor emeritus of geography at the University of Colorado, Gilbert founded the university's National Hazards Research and Applications Information Center. NAS President Bruce Alberts said, "Gil White has led major efforts in this country to significantly improve the water supplies in Africa and the Middle East."

In 1942, White presented a study of flood control management. In that same year, he began serving with the American Friends Service Committee's relief work over-

Gilbert at the celebration of AFSC's 50 years of service.

seas. His AFSC involvement continued until the 1970s, when he turned his service activities toward collborative scientific efforts, particularly on environmental issues. In an article on Quaker volunteer service in *Friends Bulletin*, Gilbert wrote: "In all of these activities I have tried, with highly variable degrees of success, to foster peaceful cooperation among contending groups, and to promote studies and collaboration in recognizing that the human race is part of the total world environment and needs to live in harmony with it."[2]

Going Deeper

Questions to Ponder

1. How does Gilbert's life speak to you?
2. How would you feel if an uncle or grandparent asked you if you expect to amount to anything? How would

---

[2] Reprinted by permission of *Quaker Life*, September 2000, page 8.

you respond? What does "amounting to something" mean to you? What might you do to amount to something?

3. Do you think people can always react to threat non-violently? Think of a particular threat and make a list of all the things you could do that would not be violent.

4. Do you think Gilbert would have done more good if he had concentrated on helping people directly instead of using science to change whole systems? Why or why not?

Activities

1. From a local newspaper, identify an unsolved problem in your area. Who are the individuals and groups that would need to work together to solve it? Find out what's being done toward solving it.

2. Is there an ROTC or Junior ROTC in your community? Are there any groups or individuals doing counter military recruitment? Why do Quakers oppose ROTC training?

3. What are some of the problems we have now in stopping the spread of nuclear weapons?

Illustration Credits

Page 128: photograph courtesy of AFSC Archives.

Page 132: photograph by Theodore B. Hetzel, courtesy of *Friends Journal*.

Page 135: photographs courtesy of John Thompson, Drawers of Water II Project, IIED, UK, and partners in East Africa.

Page 137: photograph courtesy of AFSC Archives.

Signe Wilkinson
Cartoons with a Serious Message[1]

by Signe Wilkinson and Beth Parrish

It was the ninth day of August, 1990. I was preparing to take the family to that sacred Quaker vacation spot —Maine—when the call came. "Signe, we need a cartoon in the paper to address the troops being sent by President Bush to the Persian Gulf."

Self-portrait.

I was on vacation and didn't want to think about cartoons. Since the success of a cartoon does depend on timing, however, I put my attitude aside and started working on it.

Normally, I do my cartoons at the office. I generally read several newspapers by about 9:30 AM and begin sketching many ideas on the one or two topics I'm interested in. I hope to get a good one before lunchtime. If I don't have

[1] More of Signe Wilkinson's cartoons can be found at **www.signetoons.com**.

Signe's cartoon expressing her opinion of the first President Bush sending troops to the Gulf (August, 1990).

an image by then, I get really worried. Sometimes, however, I get one done by 4:30 PM but decide to do a different, better one. Then I take my ideas to a few trusted friends on the staff of the newspaper who let me know which one they like. My editor passes on the cartoon at the end of the day after I've drawn the final version.

This time, I was at home, my subject was chosen for me, and I had to draw from what I knew about the Gulf War, Iraq's takeover of Kuwait, and the United States' response to that. Why were we going there? What did we hope to accomplish? I completed the cartoon and submitted it.

The night editor looked at my work and asked, "Are you sure you want to run this?"

Everybody needs a night editor. Getting tested daily is a good thing. I said, "Yes."

The cartoon ran the next day in the *Philadelphia Daily News* as the troops were being deployed. One hundred seventy thousand newspapers displayed my opinion on the editorial page.

Everybody seemed to be waving the flag and supporting the Middle East war that we now call the Gulf War. They all seemed to want to crush Saddam Hussein. Many watched everything they could about the war on TV. They enjoyed learning the names of all the new weapons, planes, and land vehicles.

Although my cartoon expressed dismay at the Americans for valuing unlimited consumption of world resources over lives lost in war, the *Philadelphia Daily News*, a Knight-Ridder-owned newspaper, published it. This unpopular view of the war was printed. The readership didn't revolt. The paper survived; the editor survived; I survived. I still believe what I drew. It's a good cartoon.

More from Signe As of April, 2003

My age? Middle. I have a hubbie (of 24 years) and two daughters, 18 and 14 years of age, who attend Germantown Friends School.

I started drawing as a child. My art teacher in junior high encouraged me, as did the late Sig Titone, a fantastic artist and printmaker from Willistown Friends Meeting. After high school (where I received no encouragement), I studied at the Academy of Fine Arts in Philadelphia. They trained me to draw classical statues, which helped me gain control of my style. But l didn't exactly fit their mold.

I did not start out as a cartoonist for a newspaper. In 1973, I started as a journalist, but the unbiased reporting confined me. I had illustrated some articles with cartoons and enjoyed doing that. Soon I began submitting political cartoons.

Great cartoons require a simple style, good drawing, and a clear message on critical issues. For maximum impact, a cartoon must be published at a crucial time. There is a narrow range of topics that capture an audience. People often write in response to my cartoons on Israel, war, abortion, racism, and the death penalty.

Compared to politicians, political cartoons are powerless little things. They can't give friends tax breaks, vote themselves raises, send kids off to war, or protect our private lives from government intrusion. Somehow, though, on their way from the newstand to birdcage liner, cartoons seem to incite brief incendiary bursts, propelling readers to call me for apologies or ask for reprint rights.

One of the things I learned growing up as a Quaker woman was that my opinions mattered. We Quakers underestimate the liberation that gives us. In meeting we learn that any one of us might have something good to say or contribute.

As a cartoonist or journalist I am not an activist. One's job in that kind of work is not fully one's life. My needs for activism are met by working to help restore the historic Fairhill Burial Ground in northern Philadelphia. Lucretia Mott, the famous Quaker abolitionist, is buried there. The cemetery was deserted for many years, but we bought it back and are working hard to make it into a beautiful green spot.

The neighborhood around it is called "The Badlands." Hispanics and African Americans now live in this impoverished area. When we started our cleanups, prostitutes and addicts were on the streets. There was dangerous gun crossfire. However, Quakers and non-Quakers worked there for days—repairing fences and removing syringes, whiskey bottles, trash, brambles, and weeds. We wielded chainsaws to remove unwanted treegrowth. Through Quaker process, and with the help of the neighbors in deciding what trees to plant and what else we want there, the land is now safe and green.

That is what activism is to me. "Just do it" should be the Quaker motto.[2]

More about Signe

Signe is an attender at the Chestnut Hill Meeting in Philadelphia. She is the editorial cartoonist for the *Philadelphia Daily News*. In 1992 she won the Pulitzer Prize for Editorial Cartooning. Her illustrations about Quakers grace publications from Quaker Press of Friends General Conference, *The Quaker Way* and the *Directory of Traveling Friends*.

More about the Gulf War

Kuwait is a small, very rich country just south of Iraq. After World War I, when the boundary lines were drawn, Iraq thought Kuwait should have been included in Iraq. In 1990 Iraq owed money to Kuwait. When Kuwait wouldn't forgive its debt, Iraq decided to invade Kuwait and make it part of Iraq. Signals from the United States were evidently unclear: Iraq's ruler, Saddam Hussein, thought the United States would not interfere in its conquest of Kuwait. He was wrong, of course.

On August 1, 1990 negotiations between Iraq and Kuwait collapsed and the next day Iraq's troops invaded Kuwait. The day after that, the United Nations Security Council condemned the invasion and demanded that Iraq withdraw its army from Kuwait. Saddam Hussein ignored that demand. He warned the United States not to intervene, but a few days later, on August 7, the United States sent troops to Saudi Arabia.

---

[2] Adapted slightly from Signe's book, *Abortion Cartoons on Demand*, Philadelphia, PA: Broad St. Books, 1992. You can see her cartoons online at www.signetoons.com or on the opinion pages of the *Philadelphia Daily News* at **www.Phillynews.com**.

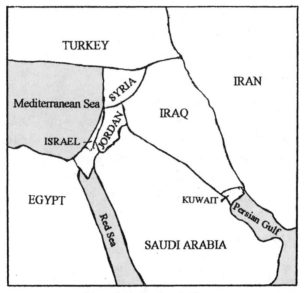

Map of the Persian Gulf area.

The next day, Iraq annexed Kuwait. It was the day after that when Signe drew her cartoon, described and shown on page 140.

In the following months, US troops were increased, but the Gulf War didn't start till mid-January, 1991. It was very short. After heavy bombing by the United States, the Iraqi army started retreating. More bombing of the retreating troops became a massacre, and the first President Bush stopped it and ended the war. He was criticized by some people later for not going on to get rid of Saddam Hussein.

Going Deeper

Questions to Ponder

1. How does Signe's life speak to you?
2. Do you have a "night editor" in your life to help you test your beliefs and actions? Who is he or she?

3. How do you feel when you express opinions and hear others strongly disagreeing with you?
4. How hard is it for you to "put your attitude aside" as Signe did when she gave up her planned vacation?

Activities

1. Pick a problem or issue that you are concerned about and create a cartoon about it.
2. Unscramble these letters to spell words from this story (answers on page 168):

TAROCOM __ __ __ __ __ __ __

SNARPEI UGFL __ __ __ __ __ __ __

__ __ __ __

EBIFEL __ __ __ __ __ __

ISPCOT __ __ __ __ __ __

DINSFER __ __ __ __ __ __ __

REDTIO __ __ __ __ __ __

Signe's cartoon showing "Uncle Sam" shooting darts at the world.

operator assisted   direct-dial Party Line

Signe's cartoon illustrating "direct-dialing" Quakers contrasted with "operator assisted" religious groups.

3. Pick a topic where there are many strong opinions. Play the devil's advocate (take a contrary point of view if it isn't your own). Find out how it feels when no one agrees with you.

Illustration Credits

Page 139: illustration courtesy of Signe Wilkinson, *The Philadelphia Daily News*.

Page 140: illustration courtesy of Signe Wilkinson, *The Philadelphia Daily News*.

Page 144: map courtesy of Marnie Clark.

Page 145: illustration courtesy of Signe Wilkinson, *The Philadelphia Daily News*.

Page 146: illustration courtesy of Signe Wilkinson, *The Quaker Way*, Quaker Press of FGC, 1998.

Violet Zaru
Hope in a Refugee Camp
by Beth Parrish

W hen she was a young girl in 1939 Violet Zaru told her teacher, Annice Carter, and the principal, Mildred White, that she wanted to become a Quaker. Her parents had enrolled her in the Ramallah Friends School in Palestine several years before, though they were Greek Orthodox. After Violet's father died when she was in the fourth grade, the principal loved and cared for Violet and her brother, Faud, as if they were her own children. As a result, both children grew very close to the staff at the school. When Violet and Faud expressed their wish to become Quakers, their mother was pleased and blessed them with the words, "Now you are in safe hands." Violet believes that the seeds of love, kindness, and strong faith that took root and bloomed in her heart were indeed planted by those great Quakers at the Ramallah Friends School.

Lessons in the Friends School

The simple lessons she learned as a student continue to be the same important values that Violet teaches to the Palestinian children she cares for today at the Quaker Play Center, in the area near Ramallah where she grew up. Violet remembers the day when the basketball team, of which she was a member, went to Jerusalem to play their final game with the team at English High School for Girls.

Violet's team won the game and the silver cup! The bus on the trip back home was full of happy girls, laughing and singing. Annice Carter and Mildred White were also aboard the bus. "Someone offered candy," Violet recalls.

We threw the candy wrappers outside through the bus windows. All of a sudden, we heard Mildred's quiet voice ordering the bus driver to stop. When he did, Mildred said, "Girls, get down and pick up all of whatever you threw out the bus windows." And of course we did.

The next day, the girls were called to the office, where Mildred asked them to sit down and then offered them some chocolates. She said with her calm, gentle voice,

Girls, I do not care whether you come back with the silver cup or not, but I care and love very much to see you keep your environment, streets, playgrounds, and wherever you may be, clean. Remember, dear girls, to put whatever you have in your hands where it belongs.

Violet learned another lesson in sewing class. The girls were sewing dresses. Violet had carefully followed her teacher's instructions to measure, cut out, and then sew the pieces together. But she couldn't finish hers because she had lost one of the sleeves. All the other girls put on their dresses to show the teacher, but Violet didn't. She was afraid, worried, and embarrassed for the terrible mistake she had made. When the teacher, Miss Carter, found out about the missing sleeve, she went to Violet, hugged her, and said,

Violet, do not be so upset. Do not feel bad. We all make mistakes. We are all human beings and human beings make mistakes. We are all children of God. And our Father, God, forgives his children.

As a Quaker, Violet participated in the activities of her meeting. In seventh grade, she and two other girls helped with Sunday School. They studied lessons and scripture with one of the Quaker women on Saturday afternoons. On Sundays the meetinghouse was quite filled by students from the Ramallah Friends School and people of many faiths from the community. The Friends welcomed them all. Gathered together, they listened to the preacher, sang hymns, and prayed together.

In 1948 the United Nations established the state of Israel in part of what had been Palestine. War broke out between the Israelis and the Palestinians, and the whole Middle East was in conflict. Many Palestinians left their homes to go to safer locations. Violet's family fled to Beirut in Lebanon and remained there for three years. Other families relocated to tent refugee camps which, over time, became more permanent accommodations and are still there. Borders between countries changed. Israel covered more of the territory, and even portions that were not part of Israel came under Israeli military control.

Love of God and of people grew in Violet despite the turmoil going on around her. In 1951 Violet's family moved back to Ramallah, where Violet returned to her Sunday School teaching activities and also did some teaching at the Friends Girls School. She spent several years in the United States attending colleges in North Carolina and South Carolina on scholarships, but after receiving her masters degree, she returned to her homeland and activities in Ramallah.

The Beginning of the Quaker Play Center

In 1974 Violet met with three women from the United Nations who were looking for a way to serve five-year-old refugee children who were preparing to enter school. Violet took them to visit some refugee camps and things were set in motion. The United Nations Relief and Works Agency for

Palestinian Refugees in the Near East (UNRWA) provided a building and grounds at the edge of the Amari Refugee Camp near Ramallah. The next year the Quaker Play Center was started there. It operated under the direction of the Ramallah Friends Meeting. Violet served on the local committee, and a few years later she became its supervisor.

The fifty children in the program at the Play Center do much of what children do in preschools and kindergartens in the United States, except these

Violet and teacher Wafia with the five-year-old children at the Quaker Play Center, Ramallah.

children are Muslim and speak Arabic. They learn songs about the local customs, villages, weather, and animals. Often the songs involve counting and hand-clapping activities. The children hear stories and play games. They learn their numbers and letters and move on to writing their names in workbooks. The see-saw, monkey bars, swings, slide, and sand box on the playground attract much attention from the children.

The Play Center is open six days a week from 7:30 AM to 12:30 PM. The children usually walk to the center with older brothers and sisters, who are on their way to the government-run school. Usually they bring their own snacks, such as Khubez bread (similar to pita bread) with tomatoes and cucumbers and maybe falafel. At times, the center provides

Quaker Play Center school yard (top). Violet and her children in the classroom.

sandwiches and milk for them. Violet sometimes gets small contributions to buy treats for the children. She explains,

> The main purpose of the Play Center was to have the five-year-old children come to an oasis of peace, true love, understanding, care, and last but not least, where they learn to love their neighbors. We hoped to keep these children away from the

loafing in the narrow paths of the camp amongst the soldiers, guns, bullets, and stones, hearing and seeing what is not for any child either to see or to hear.

Violet's prayer is "God, make us worthy of the children we serve."

Teaching Love in the Midst of Violence

The message that "God loves you" can be a difficult lesson to learn in a refugee camp. The place smells like sewage because of the poorly constructed system and broken pipes. Water use is limited. The temporary housing is cramped, drab, and inadequate. While Israeli soldiers are not always present in the camps, they arrive quickly if there is any kind of disturbance. Situations can suddenly become very dangerous for everyone in the camps. Parents are unhappy with their inability to provide for their families. Young people are restless and wonder if there is any future for them.

Jobs are hard to come by, especially since travel by Palestinians is limited. Jerusalem, a mere 15 miles from Ramallah, is off limits to most Palestinians for fear that they will retaliate for land lost to them in the war and since. Checkpoints, where soldiers monitor color-coded car tags and identification cards, are often locations for body searches and long periods of waiting. All Palestinians are suspected of being terrorists.

Map of the area around Ramallah.

Even though Israel holds the best promise for jobs, refugees seldom get the required passes to enter the area. Good medical care must be sought in surrounding countries rather than in nearby Jerusalem hospitals. Even though Violet traveled to Jerusalem for a basketball game as a child, getting permission to travel there today is difficult or impossible.

In October 2000 violence increased dramatically in the area around Ramallah. People were killed, and long curfews were enforced so that homes came to seem more like prisons. Many roads were blocked. A year later, across the Atlantic Ocean in the United States, planes were purposely crashed into buildings in New York and Washington, DC to cause destruction and chaos. Because the people who did those deeds had roots in the Middle East and were Muslims, many people around the world blamed all Muslims. The US President, George Bush, declared war on terrorism, which added to the uncertainty about the threat of war throughout the world.

In order to create a positive message of care, hope, and love, Friends United Meeting asked Friends meetings and churches in the United States to support a mission of love by sending cards and special candles to the children at the Play Center

Students from the Ramallah Friends School read the messages (left) while children in the Play Center (right) watch a video of children in the United States writing the cards.

"تحية طيبة لكل الشباب والشابات المحبين بين السلام واعطاء
الفرص لكل عباد الله"

.ברוכים הבאים לכל הנערים טרוצים שלום לכל בני עולם

Arabic (top) and Hebrew (bottom) script proclaim, "Greetings to young people who want peace and opportunity for all God's children."

and at the Friends schools in Ramallah. The children felt this love, even with the rising tensions all around them where they lived. Young children who had been drawing pictures of tanks and planes with bombs now drew pictures of doves and expressions of love. The children were happy to see the video of the children in the United States writing the cards to them and wishing them well.

In 2002 news coverage of the Israeli military bombings and tanks demolishing areas of Ramallah and nearby refugee camps filled television screens and newspapers, as did Palestinian suicide bombings that killed Israelis in shopping malls, public areas, and even school buses. Many people have been killed in these conflict-filled areas.

Fortunately, the Amari Refugee Camp has not been destroyed as this is being written. The Play School is being moved to a nicer part of the camp, where Violet will continue to create a safe, loving atmosphere in which the children can play and learn and experience God's love.

Violet loves every one of these refugee children. She teaches them that God loves them and that many others love them. She strongly believes that children learn what they live, not only at home, but also at school. She always encourages the teachers to let their actions, kindness, and love speak for them—these are stronger than words. She wants the little ones to follow in the steps of their teachers—just as she herself has done. She says,

When I was a young child, who lost my dear, loving father, there were those who loved me, the dear Quakers. My mother was a devoted Christian and loving mother who also guided our steps.

Although the Ramallah Friends Meeting now has fewer members, Violet attends faithfully and continues in its work. The Friends Schools are now on two campuses and have coeducation through 12th grade. Violet says,

> The Play Center is still going on because there are those who care to keep the Quaker Spirit at the Camp. The Play Center is a bright candle to the children in these difficult, troubled times. We are grateful to all those dear Friends/friends who lend a helping hand.

More about Friends and Ramallah

Violet Zaru continues the work of Quaker missionaries whose leadings took them to Ramallah from the United States in 1869. They started the Ramallah Friends Girls School to teach Palestinian girls over 100 years ago when there were few opportunities for girls even to attend school. Since that time, Friends have offered a consistent witness for nonviolence and peace, a commitment to education, a solid belief in basic human rights and the equality of all people.

The Friends Schools now serve both boys and girls, from the Play Center in the Amari Refugee Camp to the two campuses that educate these young people in English and Arabic through the 12th grade. There were 950 young people enrolled in these schools in the year 2000. For more information about the Friends Schools, contact Friends United Meeting, 101 Quaker Hill Drive, Richmond, Indiana 47374-1980 or through the internet at **www.fum.org** or email **missions@fum.org** or **csouth@palfriends.org** in Ramallah.

Going Deeper

Questions to Ponder

1. How does Violet's life speak to you?
2. In what ways might Violet's own childhood give her the strength and the will to remain in Ramallah to work in the Play Center under such difficult conditions?
3. Describe an event in your life that taught you an important lesson. What did you learn?
4. Do you agree with Violet that actions are stronger than words? Why or why not?

Activities

1. Find out from Friends United Meeting what the current situation is at the Play Center, Ramallah Friends School and Ramallah Friends Meeting.
2. If you wanted to visit Palestine what kind of preparations would you need to make?
3. Find out about the worldwide refugee situation. How many refugees are there in the world today? From how many different countries?

Illustration Credits

Pages 150–151: photographs by Melanie Weidner, *Quaker Life*, January/February 2002.

Page 152: map courtesy of Marnie Clark.

Page 153: photographs by Melanie Weidner, *Quaker Life*, January/February 2002.

Page 154: Arabic script courtesy of Taiyyaba Qureshi, Hebrew script courtesy of Melissa Segal.

Quaker Nobel Prize Winners

by Barbara Robinson

M ost Friends do not do good works to get praise or social recognition. Lives that speak are echoes of the Inward Guide teaching us to love. They are expressions of our testimonies for simplicity, integrity, peace, equality, and community. There have been times, however, when Quakers have received significant world recognition for the work they have done. Four times the Nobel Committee has awarded a prize to Quakers.

Emily Greene Balch (1887–1961)

In 1946, Emily Greene Balch shared the Nobel Peace Prize with John Mott of the YMCA. Emily received the award for her untiring lifelong work for peace—much of it before women got the vote. She was only the third woman to win the Nobel Peace Prize.

Growing up in a Unitarian family in the Boston area, Emily attended Bryn Mawr, a woman's college near Philadelphia started by Quakers. While at Bryn Mawr,

Emily Greene Balch.

she became interested in working for a better society. Upon graduation, she received a scholarship to spend a year studying economics at the Sorbonne in Paris, France. As part of her studies, she did research on public relief for poor people. When she returned to Boston in 1891, she helped found Denison House, one of the first settlement houses in the United States. A settlement house was a community center in an economically poor area that provided educational and social activities for neighborhood people. This work led her to involvement with labor unions, which were struggling to gain better working conditions.

Emily came to believe that teaching would enable her to make a greater contribution to improving society. She went back to school at the Harvard Annex (which became Radcliffe College) and later, at the University of Chicago and the University of Berlin, qualifying herself to teach economics and sociology. In 1900 she began to teach at Wellesley College, where she taught their first sociology course and worked on concerns related to immigration. In 1910 she published her first book, *Our Slavic Fellow Citizens*. This book won wide acclaim and is still used as a basic text today.

World War I began in 1914. Emily felt strongly that war was not the way of Christianity. Early the next year, she joined the Women's Peace Party and took a leave of absence from Wellesley College to join Jane Addams at the International Peace Congress of Women at The Hague. The women tried in vain to persuade national leaders to stop fighting and agree to a mediation process. After that, she tried to prevent the United States from entering the war, which led to her being dismissed from Wellesley College after teaching there for nearly 20 years. She joined the American Union Against Militarism and became a member of the Fellowship of Reconciliation Council.

In 1919 the women met again at The Hague, where Emily Balch and Jane Addams were co-founders of the Women's

The Women's International League of Peace and Freedom (WILPF) was organized at this 1915 International Peace Congress. Both Emily Greene Balch and Jane Addams attended.

International League for Peace and Freedom (WILPF). Emily served as secretary and treasurer. The next year, she became a Quaker, joining London Yearly Meeting[1] instead of a meeting in the United States to avoid the divisions among US Quakers. Even more than Quakers' testimonies against war, lack of a creed, and concern for social justice, she said she valued "the dynamic force of active love," which she saw being expressed in so many ways. In the next years, she set up a WILPF headquarters in Geneva, Switzerland, and worked on disarmament, drug control, and other issues that crossed national boundaries, including attempts to reform the League of Nations.

During the 1930s, Nazism was on the rise in Germany. Emily helped refugees leave Germany and find new homes and jobs elsewhere. When World War II came, she said she was "between

---

[1] Now known as Britain Yearly Meeting.

a rock and a hard place." She faced a serious moral dilemma. She thought war was wrong, but she had seen what Hitler's evil was doing to helpless people. Eventually, she decided that this war was necessary, but she kept her memberships in her peace organizations and supported young men who felt they could not fight even to get rid of Hitler. After the war, she worked on rebuilding with the International Reconstruction Corps.

Emily gave most of her Nobel peace money to WILPF. She entitled her Nobel lecture "Toward Human Unity or Beyond Nationalism." In it, she pointed out the pitfalls of nationalism and identified many strands of connectedness that she believed were moving the world toward unity. She said,

> We are not asked to subscribe to any utopia or to believe in a perfect world just around the corner. We are asked to be patient with necessarily slow and groping advance on the road forward, and to be ready for each step ahead as it becomes practicable.

Emily believed strongly that true, workable international unity would need to have a moral, human quality, not be based on the kind of raw power with which Hitler had hoped to control the world. She hoped Americans would cherish large and generous ideals for all the world's peoples.

The American Friends Service Committee (AFSC) in Philadelphia and the Friends Service Council in London

In 1947 these two Friends' organizations shared the Nobel Peace Prize for Quaker Relief and Peace work in the world over many years. After the Franco-Prussian War of 1870–1871, the British Friends War Victims Relief Committee (a forerunner of the Friends Service Council) sent help to France. Again during World War I, they sent ambulance and relief units to France and other parts of Europe. In 1917 conscientious objectors from the United States were sent to help the British Friends. The American Friends Service Committee was established at that time, originally just for overseas work. Both organizations sent food, clothing, and medical help to Eastern Europe and districts in the Soviet Union where people were suffering from famine. They also fed thousands of children in defeated Germany. In 1927 several British peace committees that had been involved in relief and rebuilding joined to form the Friends Service Council.

As Hitler rose to power, these organizations helped refugees leave Germany for new homes abroad. In 1939 after the Spanish Civil War they distributed food to people on both sides. This has always been their practice—to help people on both sides of a conflict, not to take sides. Where possible, they help people to help themselves, as in helping injured war veterans to make artificial limbs.

As early as 1912 the Nobel Committee had considered the Quakers for their peace prize. Again in the 1920s and late 1930s, they considered Friends. In 1947 they decided that the the Quakers really should have the prize, but they encountered a problem: they couldn't figure out how to give it to them. Who should receive the award? Unlike other organizations, the Religious Society of Friends has no governing body, no one leader, no centralized body or council. The yearly meetings are related, but they are independent.

The Nobel Committee learned, however, that most of the yearly meetings supported the Friends Service Council in England and the American Friends Service Committee in the United States. Then, during World War II, a delegation of Quakers from those two organizations sought and were granted a meeting with Hitler's dreaded Gestapo to arrange for taking Jewish refugees out of Germany. The Nobel Committee decided to give the award to both these service organizations, not just for their relief work but as representatives of Quakers in general.

At first, British Friends thought perhaps they shouldn't accept an award for services that they had performed under "religious concern." In the end they agreed that they could be representatives of all the Friends who had been giving so many kinds of service to people who needed it.

The Nobel Peace Prizes are awarded in Oslo, Norway, with the Norwegian king in attendance. The British Friends Service Council selected Margaret Backhouse to receive the peace prize on their behalf. The American Friends Service Committee selected Henry Cadbury, chairman of the AFSC Board, to receive the award on their behalf. This was before the days of common air travel, so passage was booked on the *SS Queen Mary*, which took several days to cross the Atlantic Ocean.

In planning for his trip, Henry Cadbury found he had a new problem. As a Quaker believing in simplicity, he had never owned a tuxedo, but he would need to wear full formal dress—white tie and tails—to the ceremony. King Haakon would be there.

Henry went to the Material Aids room where the AFSC collected donated second-hand clothes to send abroad. By great good luck, he found that the AFSC had been collecting formal wear for the Budapest Symphony Orchestra, which was planning a foreign concert tour. As members of a poor communist country, they wouldn't

Henry Cadbury attended the Nobel Peace Prize Ceremony in finery borrowed from the AFSC Material Aids room.

have such clothes either. Henry found an outfit that fit him, borrowed it for the ceremony, and took it back to the Material Aids room when he got home.

At the award ceremony, the chairman of the Nobel Committee told about many of the events in the last 300 years in which Quakers had been involved, beyond all the things that these particular two organi-

This is the Nobel Prize medal received by Henry Cadbury.

zations had done in the present century. He made it clear that the award was for the whole Religious Society of Friends and for the way in which Friends carry out their concerns. He said, "It is not the extent of their work or its practical form that is most important . . . but rather the spirit that animates their work."

Philip Noel-Baker (1889–1982)

In 1959 Philip Noel-Baker received the Nobel Peace Prize for a lifetime of work for international peace. Long before Gandhi and Martin Luther King, Jr. he was known for his non-violent approaches to conflict and for his tireless efforts to get nations to disarm.

Starting life as Philip Baker, he was born in London in 1889 to a Quaker family. His father

Philip Noel-Baker at 21.

Allen was a manufacturer by trade but actively involved in political movements to improve the living conditions of the poor. The protection of labor unions was still in the future. As a teenager Philip helped his father write political speeches. In 1909, five years before World War I, he worked with his father on an international campaign to limit the weapons of war.

Philip came to the United States to attend Haverford College for a year, then returned to Cambridge in England to Kings College. He was a good student, received academic honors, and also competed in the Stockholm Olympics in 1912. He began work at Ruskin College in Oxford in 1914, but soon World War I broke out.

Philip supported the Allies against Germany, but could not join the army. He believed his support must be active but non-violent. He was not afraid to die, but he knew he just could not kill. To resolve their dilemma, his father, his brothers, and other Quakers created the Friends Ambulance Unit. They raised money and recruited about eighty other young Quaker volunteers to go to the war in France with the British Expeditionary forces. Philip, at age 25, led the first unit. The volunteers drove ambulances carrying wounded and dying soldiers from the battle fronts to the field hospitals. It was very dangerous work. The Friends Ambulance Unit served about 100,000 soldiers in its first two years. Philip also worked with war refugees.

While Philip was working at the field hospital in Dunkirk, he met Irene Noel. She was a volunteer, running the housekeeping operation of the hospital. They were married in 1915 and later changed their last names to Noel-Baker.

Philip's experiences during the war strengthened his convictions against war. In 1919, when the war was over, he joined Lord Robert Cecil in Paris as part of a delegation to set up a peace conference. Lord Cecil was developing his idea for a "League of Nations" to prevent future wars. Philip served in many ways, helping with research and writing proposals for the league. He also served in the British House of Commons, became chair of the Labor Party, and worked at the Foreign Office (similar to our State Department).

After the League of Nations failed, he led preparatory work for the United Nations. In 1945, after World War II, he helped draft the UN Charter. He also wrote several books. The most notable one was *The Arms Race: A Program for World Disarmament*, published in 1958. In this book he shared his life's experiences and his passionate conviction that there must be worldwide disarmament. He argued that war was futile and that the need for international cooperation was urgent and increasing in our interdependent world.

Nor did he relax after winning the Nobel Peace Prize in 1959. He continued to work for international peace and disarmament until he died in 1982.

William Vickrey (1914–1996)

William Vickery.

In 1996 William Vickrey shared the Nobel Prize in Economic Science with James A. Mirrlees of Cambridge University for their contributions to the economic theory of incentives. In his 60-year career as a teacher at Columbia University, Bill Vickrey had focused on "human economics"— the effect of money on people.

Bill was born in Victoria, British Columbia, Canada but grew up in Montclair, New Jersey. He was a serious student, graduating from Phillips Academy and then Yale University, in 1935, followed by masters and Ph.D. degrees at Columbia University. In 1938 he started his long career of teaching at

Columbia, interrupted only by his service as a conscientious objector during World War II.

Led by his Quaker conscience, Bill was especially interested in social and economic change and was always involved in peace organizations and Quaker activities. Living in Scarsdale, NY as he began his teaching career, he helped start the Scarsdale Friends Meeting and was always an active member, frequently giving deeply felt vocal ministry. He was a prolific writer of books, articles, and letters to the editor. His writings in his field of economics were known for their original, innovative thinking, some of it ahead of his time, ahead of people's readiness to accept it. Columbia President George Rupp said that Bill was treasured for "the brilliance of his extraordinarily active mind and . . . his deep concern for other human beings." After he retired from teaching he kept an office on campus and continued his work there.

Other teachers and students at Columbia remember him as warm and lovable, unconcerned about his appearance, sometimes roller-skating to campus. He had a reputation for closing his eyes during meetings, apparently paying no attention, and then opening them to make an especially sensible, appropriate comment. Bill believed that public officials should regard unemployment as the most important problem, more important than concern with surpluses and deficits.

Bill received many awards and honors including an honorary Doctorate of Humane Letters from the University of Chicago in 1979 for his work in game theory and social choice theory. He became a distinguished fellow of the American Economics Association and its president in 1992. In 1996 he was elected to the National Academy of Sciences. Members of the National Academy have been recognized for original research and give scientific and technological advice to the US government. It is a great honor to be chosen. Over the years, Bill also served as a consultant to the United

Nations and to the governments of India, Japan, Liberia, and Venezuela. He was to have received another honorary degree from the University of Toulouse in France in 1997.

Bill was thrilled when the Nobel Committee announced that he had won the Nobel Prize. He said he hoped that winning this prize would give him the "chance to spread some economic sense into the nonsense world." Now, at last, the public would listen to him.

It was not to be. Three days after news of the prize was announced, he died while driving to a meeting of the Taxation Resources, Economics and Development Conference, an organization he had co-founded that deals with the economics of modern cities—the heart of how Bill was trying to help people by making their lives more workable economically.

As a past recipient of the Nobel Peace Prize, the AFSC gets to nominate someone for the prize each year. Three of the candidates that AFSC has nominated have been given the award: John Boyd Orr, Chairman of the British National Peace Council, Dag Hammarskjold, second Secretary-General of the United Nations, and Martin Luther King, Jr., civil rights leader.

Illustration Credits

Page 157: photograph courtesy of Swarthmore College Peace Collection, Swarthmore, PA and *Friends Journal.*

Page 159: photograph courtesy of Swarthmore College Peace Collection, Swarthmore, PA.

Page 162: photograph courtesy of AFSC Archives.

Page 163 (top): photograph courtesy of AFSC Archives.

Page 163 (bottom): photograph courtesy of the Library of the Religious Society of Friends in Britain.

Page 165: photograph courtesy of Columbia University, New York, NY.

Answers to the puzzle on page 38:

Answers to the puzzle on page 145:

TAROCOM is CARTOOM

EBIFEL is BELIEF

DINSFER is FRIENDS

SNARPEI UGFL is PERSIAN GULF

IPSCOT is TOPICS

REDTIO is EDITOR